WALKING IN THE FOOTSTEPS OF JESUS

I have been privileged to travel to Israel three times—but I've never gone with Wayne Stiles. After reading his book, I felt that Wayne had taken me on a fourth. I'll be candid with you: I didn't expect this book to be this good. Don't get me wrong, I thought it would be an interesting read, but I found it to be absolutely captivating. Wayne is a great storyteller, but he is also a very careful Bible scholar. That is a very lethal combination—"lethal" in the sense that it will destroy any inclination that you have to drift off into boredom. This is a volume to be enjoyed and savored, and at times it will cause you to say, "Wow!" This travelogue is a first-class seat in an air-conditioned Mercedes bus, just like the ones that you'll find in Israel. I know you're going to enjoy the ride.

STEVE FARRAR
Bestselling author and founder of Men's Leadership Ministries

Walking in the Footsteps of Jesus is part travel guide, part memoir and part biblical commentary. Wayne takes readers on a heart-engaging pilgrimage that reveals how the places of biblical history communicate as much as the characters and stories that made their settings famous.

SANDRA GLAHN, ThM
Editor-in-chief, Kindred Spirit *magazine*
Author of the Coffee Cup Bible Study series

Wayne Stiles give us an up-close and very personal look at Christ and the Bible in *Walking in the Footsteps of Jesus.* This is a wonderful book that will not only take you back but also thrust you forward in your journey with the Savior.

DR. JACK GRAHAM
Pastor of Prestonwood Baptist Church

For twenty-first-century Westerners, grasping the time, the place, the *feel* of the Gospels is almost impossible. Our culture is too different, our lives too far removed from first-century Israel to imbibe fully the actions, the teachings, the person of Jesus as recorded in these four accounts. In his latest book, Wayne Stiles masterfully bridges that gap for us. He walks us through the places Jesus walked, helping us see what He and the disciples saw, feel what they felt, and react as they reacted.

DAVID GREGORY
Author of Dinner with a Perfect Stranger

If you've never had the opportunity to visit Israel, this book will take you there. If you expect to go soon, it will be an invaluable resource. If you've been already, Wayne's firsthand accounts and anecdotes will spark memories that will make you want to go back. But above all, the greatest accomplishment of this book is that through the backdrop of Jesus' home and humanity, you will see the mission and the glory of the suffering Savior who walked this earth in places we can still touch today.

GREG LAURIE
Pastor of Harvest Christian Fellowship
Evangelist of the Harvest Crusades

In *Walking in the Footsteps of Jesus*, Wayne Stiles gives his readers great insights into the places where Jesus walked and the thoughts Jesus must have had as He moved about the Holy Land. Few realize how formative geography was on the events and in the lives of those whom Jesus met and touched. To think of Jesus and the disciples cresting the Mount of Olives and realize what a different vista each saw while looking at the same scene will give you insight into the ways we see the vistas of our lives. *Walking in the Footsteps of Jesus* is a unique way to see Jesus, the Gospels, and the modern Holy Land through the eyes of an astute observer of all three.

DR. BILL LAWRENCE
President, Leader Formation International

WAYNE STILES

WALKING IN THE FOOTSTEPS OF JESUS

A JOURNEY THROUGH THE LANDS AND LESSONS OF CHRIST

Regal

From Gospel Light
Ventura, California, U.S.A.

Published by Regal
From Gospel Light
Ventura, California, U.S.A.
www.regalbooks.com
Printed in the U.S.A.

Photos on pages 16 and 38 by James Foo. Photos on pages 66, 67, 119, 168, 169, 172 and 173 by Wayne Stiles. Photo on page 39 by Todd Turner.

Library of Congress Cataloging-in-Publication Data
Stiles, Wayne.
Walking in the footsteps of Jesus : a journey through the lands and
lessons of Christ / Wayne Stiles.
p. cm.
Includes indexes.
ISBN 978-0-8307-4661-3 (hard cover)
1. Jesus Christ—Travel. 2. Bible. N.T. Gospels—Geography. 3. Palestine—Description
and travel. 4. Israel—Description and travel. 5. Palestine—Antiquities. 6. Christian
life—Meditations. I. Title.
BT303.9.S75 2008
225.9'1—dc22
2008010907

1 2 3 4 5 6 7 8 9 10 / 15 14 13 12 11 10 09 08

Rights for publishing this book outside the U.S.A. or in non-English languages are
administered by Gospel Light Worldwide, an international not-for-profit ministry.
For additional information, please visit www.glww.org, email info@glww.org, or write
to Gospel Light Worldwide, 1957 Eastman Avenue, Ventura, CA 93003, U.S.A.

AND HE WAS SAYING TO THEM ALL,
"IF ANYONE WISHES TO COME AFTER ME,
HE MUST DENY HIMSELF,
AND TAKE UP HIS CROSS DAILY
AND FOLLOW ME."

LUKE 9:23

CONTENTS

ACKNOWLEDGMENTS

When I finished my book, *Going Places with God*, Steve Lawson at Regal Books challenged me to get busy writing a book-length travelogue of my travels to the Holy Land. At first, I admit, the prospect seemed about as exciting as enduring someone's slides of their vacation to Galveston.

But as I thought more about how the book could take shape around a special theme—a travelogue of my journeys through the life, lands and lessons of Jesus—my hesitation changed to passion. I appreciate Steve's vision and challenge for me to write the book as well as Regal's enthusiasm to publish more of my ramblings.

In putting together these pages, I have stood on the shoulders of many who have imparted the life of Christ to me—both by instruction and by example. This book is more a product of them than me.

I'm eternally grateful to Walt Stephens and Dr. Charles Wisdom, who sat a little boy down one day and explained about sin and salvation through Christ. That day in the church office remains my earliest memory of faith in Jesus, so I reckon it as the day it happened. I'll never forget Walt's recent words as his wife, Sherry, lay across the room, dying of cancer. With the final days ebbing from her fragile life, he told me, "I never knew I could have such peace." Utter turmoil on the outside, but absolute peace on the inside—I then caught a glimpse of how Jesus must have lived, especially as He faced that dark hour at Gethsemane.

I appreciate Mel Sumrall and Tom Nelson for teaching a young man that the Bible is more than a Sunday ornament—"For it is not an idle word for you," to quote Moses, "indeed it is your life" (Deut. 32:47).

Thanks to Dr. Howard Hendricks, who instructed me to ask when studying the Bible, "*Where* did the action take place?" I never knew that the answer to that question would prove so significant in my life.

Thanks to Dr. J. Dwight Pentecost, who first taught me the life of Christ in such a way that my Bible became one book and not just two Testaments; I'll never forget the moment that clicked. During this project, I kept as my constant companion a number of harmonies of the gospels, but none proved as valuable as Dr. Pentecost's arrangement in *A Harmony of the Words and Works of Jesus Christ*.

Most dates and orders of events in this volume are the result of the meticulous scholarship of Dr. Harold Hoehner and his invaluable study found in his *Chronological Aspects of the Life of Christ*, for which I am very grateful.

Thanks to Sandra Glahn, who once gave me advice on writing that I use every time I write—unless I am being moved not to. I appreciate her keen eye for detail and the editorial skills she weilded on my manuscript.

I am grateful to Mark Sweeney for pointing me in a direction he knew was best—even when I questioned it. I thank him for believing in what God can do through my writing enough to represent me.

My trips to the lands of the Bible became life-changing journeys because of the presence of capable guides, most especially Todd Bolen, Dr. Charlie Dyer and Amir Tsarfati. Those tours also required the arrangement of countless details of travel, for which I appreciate Steve Dick of Inspiration Cruises and Tours; the Israel Bible Extension of The Master's College; Samuel Smadja of Sar-El Tours; and Mike, Cheri and Michelle Fitzsimmons of Morning Star Tours.

Thanks to Chuck and Cynthia Swindoll and Insight for Living for having the vision to take God's people to God's land—and for allowing Cathy and me to contribute so many times.

Thanks to Todd Bolen for his friendship and vital contribution to my manuscript. His critical eyes weeded my words of geographical and historical crabgrass.

Thanks to Dr. John Henderson for his friendship and wisdom; I hope he hears himself in this book and receives back the encouragement he has given.

To the Saturday morning "Hood" Bible study—Mark Atchison, Tommy Bosworth, Jimmy Harris, Steve Jester, Leon McMinn, Gus

Moreno, Greg Pihl and John Schwartz—I'm thankful for their commitment to Christ, to their families, to each other and for keeping me honest.

To my daughters, Sarah and Katie—I'm frequently amazed at their compassion, discipline and biblical observations and questions that reveal the life of Christ in them. I'm thankful for the example they both are to me in so many ways.

Admiration and genuine awe go to Cathy, my bride of almost 20 years, who walks alongside me daily as I slowly and painstakingly become more like Jesus. It's a long journey, I know. I thank her for the honor of taking it with me.

"Words are stupid things," wrote Socrates, and I agree. Words remain inadequate to express my gratefulness to the Lord Jesus for living a life so worthy to follow, for dying a death that should have been mine, for rising again as a promise of my resurrection, for allowing me to walk in His footsteps (both physically and spiritually), and for leading me to write about it.

WELCOME TO A STRANGE WORLD

The Israeli security agent glanced back and forth between me and my passport.

"This is you?" Her question caught me by surprise, and I stiffened.

"It is . . . yes." She said nothing for a few awkward moments and then narrowed her gaze for a closer look. After shuffling some papers and turning to a blank page in my passport, the young woman stamped it and handed it to me in one motion.

"You look better now," she said matter-of-factly and waved me on. I wasn't sure whether to thank her or feel insulted. As I walked away, I looked closely at my seven-year-old passport's picture for the first time in years. It did seem a bit dated—then I had large glasses and longer hair and looked like a cross between John Denver and Jerry Lewis. *At least I look better now.*

Relieved, I approached the baggage claim area at Tel Aviv's Ben Gurion Airport, feeling a bit like Agag after the battle with Saul: "Surely the bitterness of death is past" (1 Sam. 15:32). But like Agag, I was wrong.

The airline I took from America to Israel promoted the speed of one of its trans-Atlantic flights with a sign that boasted, "Breakfast in London—Lunch in New York." But I heard that some wag had spray-painted an additional line: "Baggage in Bermuda." The graffiti proved prophetic. Everyone else scuttled away from the conveyor belt with luggage in tow, and I stood there empty-handed. Then the belt stopped.

I had always thought that men who lost their luggage and whined about it were wimps. Wimps no longer. Soon I would be suffering for the Lord in a foreign land—and so would those who had to be around me!

The airline gave me a voucher worth 200 shekels to tide me over until they located my bags. Sounds like a lot, but it totaled only about 50 bucks. With more than three weeks ahead of me in Israel and an indefinite arrival time of my worldly possessions, the modest voucher reduced my shopping list to the essentials: a change of clothes and as much clean underwear as I could afford.

Once in Jerusalem, I caught a taxi to a shopping center south of the city. The mall sat in the Valley of Rephaim where David faced the Philistines more than once (see 2 Sam. 5:18,22; 23:13). The Jerusalem mall looked like American malls: same name brands, same logos, same food court . . . but the signs read in Hebrew (did you know Ronald McDonald speaks Hebrew?)—and the prices are about double. Welcome to the Middle East.

Some days later, at the moment someone announced, "Wayne, your luggage arrived," I'm not sure I would have felt any happier if he had told me that my wife had just had a son. I had almost run out of film. My supply of essentials I had purchased at the mall was dwindling to a critical level. I had run out of ways to wear the same clothes (inside out, right-side out, upside down). My feet had blisters from wearing just sandals. I never felt so happy to see two suitcases.

I opened my bags and slipped into my socks and Rockport shoes—and oh, foot heaven! I think I even slept in my shoes that night. How did they ever make it in Jesus' day without walking shoes and comfy cotton socks?

—m—

On Jesus' first trip to Israel, He had no luggage either. He came with only a confidence in His Father—and left with the same. He traveled light, trusting God to guide and provide along the journey.

Between Jesus' birth in Bethlehem and His ascension near Jerusalem, He experienced dozens of divine appointments with people whose lives, locations and longings prepared them for an encounter with a Jesus they never expected. A lonely woman in Samaria. A den of hypocrites in the Temple. A Pharisee still searching for truth. Fishermen with a sea of false expectations. A hometown ashamed of Him. And a blind man who saw more than most. Along the way, Jesus was misunderstood, misquoted, misrepresented—and often, just plain missed!

God could have chosen any number of ways to reveal Himself to us, and in the past, He did just that (see Heb. 1:1-2). But now, God has revealed Himself through His Son, and His Son through the Scriptures. In traveling to Israel, I hoped to understand the Scriptures better, and so to better understand Jesus. But I wanted more than understanding— I wanted to mingle my experiences with His.

Author Alister McGrath noted that an over-emphasis on knowledge ignores the benefits of imagination, experience and emotion. Read his words carefully:

> I had thought that we were meant to increase our factual knowledge of events. For example, when reading a text about the ministry of Jesus in Galilee, it was important to be able to find Galilee on a map, understand its cultural history, see how this fitted into the general patterns of Jesus' ministry, and even try to date the event. Yet this led to nothing more than the accumulation of facts. It did not excite or challenge me. . . . I had to think of myself as being there, witnessing what is said and done. . . . No longer was I simply registering ideas as I read. I was reliving the historical events on which my faith was grounded.[1]

Imagine following Jesus along the road, listening in on His conversations and gleaning the lessons He taught in the holy places He traveled. Picture yourself reliving the historical events that undergird your faith. This volume takes such a journey.

—⁓—

This book is a travelogue. It represents a number of my trips to the Middle East in no certain order—tours with my wife, with our daughters and by myself. But rather than make my journeys the whole basis of this book, we'll follow instead the life of Jesus, step by step. Through the lens of my experiences, we will witness His life, His lands and the lessons He taught there. We will add emotion and experience to exposition and understanding.

I never intended this volume to represent every place Jesus went or every event and conversation He had—though I mention many of these. Nor does this represent some kind of definitive chronology of the life of Christ. Instead, when you finish this journey with me, you will have a general and orderly grasp of Jesus' life and ministry. But more importantly, you'll better appreciate His unusual method in shaping the lives of those who follow Him—including your own.

As I think back on my exchange with that passport security guard, I like to imagine her asking me a different set of questions.

"Tell me, Mr. Stiles, did you come to Israel for business or pleasure?"

"Well, uh . . . neither really, I guess."

"Oh? So why did you come to the Holy Land?"

"I'm . . . looking forward to seeing the places Jesus walked, and—"

"And are you *worthy* to walk in the footsteps of Jesus?"

"Well, uh . . . no . . . I'm—"

"I see. So after you have seen those holy places, after you have taken your pictures, what difference will it all make to you?"

I would love if those questions were really asked of tourists.

As I discovered, walking the land where Jesus walked offers little more than dirty feet unless the lessons of those sacred places find their way into our hearts.

The Christian life is a journey, not just a destination. And unfortunately, God doesn't give us walking shoes and cotton socks for our journey with Jesus. We wear sandals. Our walk includes dirty feet, pebbles under our heels, blisters, potholes, detours, stumbles—and lost luggage. But ultimately, even surprisingly, we always arrive where God wants us to go. It just never happens the way we expected.

That first day in Israel was not at all what I anticipated. Instead of a great spiritual experience, I found myself in a mall in the Valley of Rephaim, trying to figure out how to say in Hebrew, "Excuse me. Where can I buy some clean underwear?"

I came to Israel to walk in the footsteps of Jesus. But like those who followed Him along the dusty roads of His day, I had no real idea of the journey I was about to take.

Note

1. Alister E. McGrath, *The Journey: A Pilgrim in the Lands of the Spirit*, 1st ed. (New York: Doubleday, 2000), pp. 16-18.

Running in the wilderness where the Hebrews
wandered for 40 years with the Tabernacle of God.

CHAPTER ONE

CAMPING WITH JESUS

And the Word became flesh, and dwelt among us, and we saw His glory.
JOHN 1:14

Bethlehem seemed a bit boring at first. But then, I'm not much of a shopper.

In the city of Jesus' birth, we spent the bulk of our time, I confess, in a tourist shop. Gold jewelry set with opals and diamonds sat alongside bowls, oil lamps and other imitation artifacts. Olive-wood statues filled the interior of the large establishment, coloring the whole room light brown. Name any biblical character or animal, and there was an olive-wood statue for you! Favorites included Samson pushing the pillars, David slaying Goliath and, of course, Nativity scenes of every shape, size and price—from a few bucks to a few thousand. And the tourists fell upon the plunder.

I examined one wooden figurine and flipped it over: "Made in China." Another caught my eye, a bust of Elvis Presley, and I had to grin. *Elvis in Israel?* I called over the owner, a proprietor who can smell a tour bus a mile away, and asked him my question. He corrected me.

"That's Joseph Smith."

"Oh . . . I see." I had never before noticed the resemblance between the king of rock 'n' roll and the founder of Mormonism. I guess the upturned collar threw me. The owner could see my disappointment and promptly offered a solution.

"But if you like, it's Elvis!"

Bethlehem's main attraction centers on the oldest standing church in Israel, which marks the traditional site of Jesus' birth. Built in the sixth century by the emperor Justinian, the Church of the Nativity sits on top of beautiful mosaics from the original church that Constantine's mother, Helena, constructed just a few centuries after Christ. Early and strong tradition supports that Mary gave birth to Jesus in the cave

17

beneath the church—and a star on the ground today even marks the traditional spot of the Nativity, which means "the Birth."

In front of the church, a large courtyard called Manger Square accommodates pilgrims who gather every Christmas Eve. The traditional Western celebration begins on December 24, followed by the Greek Orthodox Christmas on January 6 and the Armenian observance almost two weeks later.

Today, Bethlehem claims over 30,000 residents—hardly the "little town" of Jesus' day. Construction continues in the outskirts and remains a frequent source of political strife. The distant jackhammering sounds like a roller coaster clanking up its first big climb.

Our tour group bussed just east of the city to a large pasture called "The Shepherds' Field"—the traditional site of the angels' announcement. A deep breath felt great; here the events of the Savior's birth seemed more authentic. Here we exchanged Christmas shopping for the Christmas story. No olive-wood statues . . . just olive trees. No merchants hawking trinkets . . . just some local Palestinian children holding lambs in their arms for us to pet. I couldn't help but think of a young David, who kept his father's flocks in the fields nearby.

Our Christian guide told us that the shepherds of that first Christmas guarded flocks raised for sacrifice in Jerusalem. If so, the words they heard from the herald—"Today in the city of David there has been born for you a Savior, who is Christ the Lord" (Luke 2:11)—gave a glimpse of what salvation would cost: The babe in the manger would become the final sacrificial lamb. Jesus was born to die in Jerusalem only five miles up the road—just like the flocks the shepherds pastured that night.

Caves punctured the slopes of this pastoral scene. I entered one cave with a rock wall partially filling its mouth, with a narrow opening for passage. Built by some modern shepherd, the wall offered shelter and security for his flock. By sleeping in the gap, the shepherd served as the "gate"—a custom also common in Jesus' day, which He used to illustrate the secure salvation He offers: "I am the gate; whoever enters through me will be saved. He will come in and go out, and find pasture. My sheep listen to my voice; I know them, and they follow me. I give them eternal life, and they shall never perish; no one can snatch them out of my hand" (John 10:9,27-28, *NIV*).

I squinted past the sun to the warm sky above me. I tried to picture the star over Bethlehem and the glory of the Lord that illumined this field that night, as bright as the daylight in which I stood.

As I glanced to the southeast, I spied the Herodium—the flat-topped, manmade mountain fortress Herod the Great had built for himself. After the magi told the paranoid king that the "King of the Jews" had been born, Herod tried to slay Jesus by killing the boys of Bethlehem. But instead, God told Joseph in a dream to take Jesus and Mary and flee to Egypt. (This wasn't the first Joseph, by the way, whom God spoke to in dreams and sent to Egypt.) In a wonderful twist of poetic irony, the raving King Herod died and was buried in the Herodium—where archaeologists recently discovered his tomb—overlooking the birthplace of the true King of Israel.

The wonder of God's power must have seemed a cruel contradiction to the conditions Joseph and Mary found upon entering Bethlehem. Imagine traveling south 60 hard miles only to find no room in the inn. Two thousand years of waiting for the Messiah, and He's born in a barn and laid in a feed trough! Why would God choose such an ignoble beginning for such an important birth? (Probably the same reason God would choose such an ignoble death for such an exemplary life.) *We* would have given God's Son a room in the finest five-star hotel in Bethlehem. But Jesus got only a one-star motel—and God had to provide the star!

Since that day in the field, I've never been able to croon "O Little Town of Bethlehem" the same way; now, all Christmas carols seem historical rather than just traditional. Ever since I walked the place of their inspiration, they have become songs of worship. The change was surprising—a gift I enjoy each Christmas.

As we left The Shepherds' Field, the children who had held the lambs for us to pet now held out their hands for coins. We obliged.

—∞—

As we headed south through the Negev, we stopped in Beersheba and scattered for a meal. Several of us squeezed into a small eatery with two or three tables. The lady behind the counter spoke up before taking my order. "You're American?"

"Yes," I nodded.

"And from Texas," she added. This surprised me, because I don't have a Southern twang or wear boots or big belt buckles.

"Right again," I smiled. "How in the world did you know?"

"You're wearing a cowboy hat."

In Israel, a hat ranks high on the list of basics, especially down south. But not everyone understands the reasons for a hat. One guy in our group wore his baseball cap backward, bill in the back, the whole trip. Within two days, his squinted face glowed a bright red, but he never turned the cap around.

My straw hat, on the other hand, would have worked whichever way I wore it. It gave shade all around and allowed the breeze to blow through. But it *wasn't* a cowboy hat; it was Australian. My wife, Cathy, tells me the hat makes me look like Indiana Jones, an association I much prefer to a cowpoke.

"It's not a cowboy hat," I objected. "It's Australian." She looked again.

"It's a cowboy hat. Your order, please?" She guessed I came from Texas by the Australian straw hat I wore!

I grew up in San Antonio, a city with the same latitude as Timna Park, Israel, which is just north of Eilat and the Red Sea. Hundred-degree Texas days bullied me like the kid across the street, but the Arabah Valley of Israel throws a harder punch. Especially from the Dead Sea south to the Red Sea, this valley burns hotter than any Texas summer I remember.

As I gulped water from my CamelBak in Timna Park, drinking seemed as useful as pouring water on the ground. What a place. Scrubby acacia trees scattered around offered no shade; they reminded me of the thorny, leafless mesquite trees of Texas. Large, steep sandstone formations interrupted the otherwise flat desert, jutting up red and dark as if burnt from exposure above ground. And did I mention the forecast? *Hot.*

The park offers a few fascinating features, including displays on the history of ancient copper mining and remnants of Egyptian idol worship. The most famous attraction boasts the name Solomon's Pillars. But don't be fooled. Like Solomon's Pools near Bethlehem and Solomon's Stables beneath Jerusalem's Temple Mount, these Nubian sandstone pillars in Timna Park—while beautiful—have nothing to do with King Solomon. Like a celebrity endorsement, just slap on the name and tourists come for miles.

For me, the park's real significance centered on something modern, not ancient. A Baptist organization had constructed a scale model of the Tabernacle that Moses carried around in this same wilderness for 40 years. Once in Eureka Springs, Arkansas, I saw another scale model of the Tabernacle, but that fiberglass structure looked more like a piece of modern art. The one in Timna Park looked like the real thing.

Skeptics have come to inspect the dimensions of the Tabernacle model at Timna only to find that it faithfully reproduces the proportions given in Exodus 35–40. But reading the description in Exodus can't compare to standing outside what looked like the Tabernacle itself—and in the same wilderness! I felt as if I had walked through a doorway of history.

Even though this Tent of Meeting offered a great glimpse of biblical history and could potentially attract a greater number of tourists, Israeli park information and most tour books mysteriously omit the Tabernacle's presence in the park. Why? Probably because the Baptists are quick to point out to Christian tourists how the Tabernacle foreshadowed Jesus Christ. The book of Hebrews does the same (see Heb. 9:8-12).

A soft-voiced college student walked our group to the front of the model. Dressed in period costume with Velcro sandals, he explained the history of the Exodus in such slow detail that some of us grew concerned for the elderly who stood in the heat. Beads of sweat formed on foreheads, water bottles opened and emptied, and people clustered in bits of shade as if sharing an umbrella during a downpour.

As I watched the white curtains billowing around the perimeter of this Tabernacle, the ropes stretching out, staked to the unspoiled desert where the original tent stood—one event dominated my thinking. Christmas.

Matthew and Luke record the stories we read each December, but John's account states the event so succinctly that no Christmas play could use it as its text: "And the Word became flesh, and dwelt among us, and we saw His glory" (John 1:14). The three-part crescendo begins with the inconceivable miracle of the virgin birth (really, the virgin *conception*): God became man.

The term John uses for "dwelt" stems from a word meaning "tabernacle." In other words, God became a man "and *tabernacled* among us." The beloved apostle clearly compares the wilderness Tabernacle with Jesus' life in the flesh. John climaxes his statement by saying that the same glory that filled the Tabernacle in the wilderness, the same presence of the Lord, also dwelt among men in the Man, Jesus Christ—still fully God but now also fully man.

Jesus camped with us. And I stood in front of the perfect metaphor.

—⚊—

Our journey through the lands and lessons of Christ begins by understanding that God's presence among His people took place long before Jesus came to Earth. Like the star that penetrated Bethlehem's dark sky, God's glory has pierced the dark pages of history again and again at significant points. As we follow the movement of God's glory in this chapter from Eden to the Tabernacle to the Temple to Jesus, we see that history reveals itself as *His story*—and His is a story of redemption.

When Adam and Eve ate the forbidden fruit, they knew instinctively that God can't abide sin in His presence, so they hid from Him. God then sacrificed an animal to atone for their sin and cover their nakedness (see Gen. 3:8,21). So began the major problem the whole Bible sets out to solve: God wants us but not our sin. God wants to dwell with His people, but our sin gets in the way. It's that simple. Our sin had to be removed.

The Tabernacle provided a major step forward in God's plan of redemption. It supplied a way for a holy God to deal with sin and, at the same time, to dwell with His people. It also foreshadowed how the Lord would ultimately deal with sin once and for all: He would *tabernacle* with us.

As I did in Bethlehem with the star, I lifted my eyes to the back of the Tabernacle and pictured the pillar of cloud and fire that hovered over it in Moses' day, giving a visual testimony that God dwelt with His people (see Exod. 40:34-38). God told Moses to build the Tabernacle so that He might dwell among His people. He *wanted* to tabernacle with them (see Exod. 25:8; 29:46; Lev. 26:11-12). Even though the Lord concealed His glory inside the tent, the cloud that lingered above it served to remind the people that God dwelt with them. The pillar of cloud reminds me of when the Union Jack flies over Windsor Castle or Buckingham Palace, signifying that the queen is in residence. One glance put all wonders to rest: *God is with us.* How gracious a reassurance.

While the soft-spoken Baptist brother waxed on about the Exodus and the placement of the priests and tribes around the Tabernacle, I worked my way to the entrance of the tent until I stood right beside it. Unnoticed, I drew back the dark curtains and slipped inside. Suddenly, I was all alone.

23

The courtyard seemed bigger inside than out. The fabric walls flapped in the wind, held fast by wooden poles around the perimeter. The abundance of acacia wood in the Sinai Peninsula provided the framing material for the construction of the biblical Tabernacle's poles and furniture. This plentiful hardwood even had a place named after it, Shittim (see Josh. 2:1).

The simple white cloth served as one of several critical barriers between the people and God—a necessary separation. Today, no ordinary citizen who travels to Washington, DC, would expect to barge into the Oval Office and chat with the president. Very few enjoy that kind of access. When my family took a simple tour of the White House, we had to send our identification weeks ahead of time, and our visit was restricted to certain rooms on the first floor. The hierarchy of government sets apart its highest officials.

The Tabernacle did this with God, showing Him as "set apart"—the meaning of the word "holy." Interestingly, the president's separation from the people protects *the president*. But in ancient Israel, God's separation protected *the people*. No one, not even the most pious, would dare to enter the presence of God by themselves. The punishment was certain death—a penalty still in effect, by the way (see Rom. 6:23).

As I stood alone in the courtyard, I experienced a moment the ancient Israelite never would have experienced. *Ever*. You *never* entered alone. And when you did come, it wasn't for a tour or for snapshots. You came for business—to make right your relationship with a holy God.

What blocked my path made this clear. Immediately before me stood a large, bronze altar, chest high, seven and a half feet square, with red paint that looked like blood on the horns that protruded from each of four corners. Sometimes called the "brazen altar," this imposing structure made plain that the only way to God came through the death of a sacrifice as a substitute for the death of the sinner. All sacrifices began with "the burnt offering," from the Hebrew word *olah* (see Lev. 1:3). We get the English word "holocaust" (meaning "burnt whole") from the Greek transliteration of *olah*. Everything goes up in smoke—an essential and illustrative fact that the consequences of sin require death. The altar represented the place where your sacrifice died in your place. You walked in, and there the altar stood. There was no getting around it.

With all the pizzazz of a great pyrotechnics show, fire came from God and consumed the first sacrifice made on the altar (see Lev. 9:24). And God commanded the priests to keep His flames burning continually, signifying continual access to Him.

Standing where the smell of sacrifices would have changed from barbecue to burnt, I imagined myself without Christ, relying on the frail integrity of my human priest and the smoldering sacrifice I would have brought. It was not a good feeling. I prefer Jesus, knowing His perfect work on the cross has satisfied all of what this Tabernacle represented.

"Please"—a voice outside the curtain interrupted my thoughts—"you need to come out."

I hadn't had permission to enter the courtyard—a fact, I later realized, that represented a microcosm of the whole theology I had just been thinking about. No one dared enter God's presence alone, without permission, without a priest and without a sacrifice.

I rejoined the group in time to hear the young guide explain the completion of the Tabernacle's construction recorded at the end of the book of Exodus. To my relief, he didn't continue with Leviticus, and we turned to enter the Tabernacle again, this time as a group.

We passed the brazen altar and the bronze laver (or washbowl) where the priests would have washed their hands, and we stood before the entrance to the Holy Place. The exposed topside of the tent looked dull and drab, but the flaps underneath revealed white, blue and red cherubim, beautifully embroidered into the fabric. Outside unremarkable, inside extraordinary—again, just like Jesus.

As we entered the Holy Place inside the tent, a place only priests could have entered, the brightness of day vanished. My eyes adjusted, and on the right I saw the Table of Showbread, holding 12 loaves to represent the 12 tribes of Israel. I touched a loaf—hard plastic (but most European bread feels that way anyway). On the left stood the menorah, or candle stand, which offered the only light to the dark room. With no breeze, the airless room felt stifling, like a summer attic. At the back of the Holy Place, the continual burning on the Altar of Incense would have only added to the heat.

Behind the altar, we drew back the veil and entered the Most Holy Place, the Holy of Holies. Immediately a blast of cold, fresh air hit us. Air conditioning! (Some American must have thought of that.) We crammed our grateful group into the small room and encircled its only piece of furniture, a replica of the Ark of the Covenant. Golden angels faced each other over what would have been in the original a solid gold lid, the Mercy Seat. Here, the very presence of God would have dwelt as bright as the sun, called the *Shechinah* glory, from a Chaldee term meaning "resting place." The words "mercy seat" come from a Hebrew word related to *Kippur*—"to make atonement."

Once a year on the Day of Atonement, or Yom Kippur, the high priest would sprinkle goat blood on the Mercy Seat to atone for sins, cleanse the Tabernacle and make a way for God to remain dwelling among a sinful people. The whole purpose of the sacrifice was *atonement*—our translation of the word "atonement" stems from a thirteenth-century English term meaning "at-one-ment." The rite brought the believer back into fellowship with God (see Lev. 16:16). But this kind of fellowship, though gracious, was frightful. One wrong move and you're dead.

Standing over the Ark of the Covenant that day, I felt somewhat like Indiana Jones (especially with my hat on). But when the tour leader pulled back the lid for us to look inside at replicas of Aaron's rod, a jar of manna and two tablets—even though I knew these were reproductions—I felt uneasy. Most remember the scene in *Raiders of the Lost Ark* where the curious Nazis die creative deaths after looking inside the Ark. But fewer remember where such an event happened for real!

—⚬—

Far north of Timna Park, near another site called Timnah, the western breezes wafted up the Sorek Valley to the site of Beth-Shemesh. After Israel settled in the land of Canaan, they set up the Tabernacle at Shiloh. But the Philistines captured the Ark in battle, eventually returning it on a cart that traveled east along an ancient road toward the site on which I stood—Beth-Shemesh. I could see in the distance where this road had been in the Sorek Valley. Railroad tracks lay there today. When the Ark arrived at Beth-Shemesh, some of the men chanced a curious peek inside. Bad idea. Insert that scene from *Raiders* here (see 1 Sam. 6:19).

Turning to my right, or northeast, I saw the nearby sites of Zorah and Eshtaol, where the judge Samson grew up. His carnal curiosity took him the other way down the Sorek Valley—west toward Timnah, to Philistine women. I had to marvel at the contrasting curiosities of both Samson and the men of Beth-Shemesh: one a curiosity about sin and the others a curiosity about holiness. But the first makes the second just as deadly.

Farther north, the shade of an olive-tree grove offered us a pleasant place for a picnic. Our bus driver's wife had put together a simple sack lunch for each of us. I opened mine and found a pita cut in two, one half filled with lunch meat, the other with cheese. Most things in Israel seem to come in a pita. (I half-expected my room key in a pita.) A green banana, a whole tomato, a raw cucumber and my sack was empty. We bought water to drink. Local schoolchildren ate their lunches on the ground just opposite us, their colorful backpacks set aside on their field trip to ancient Shiloh.

The name "Shiloh" existed long before the Civil War battle or the Neil Diamond song. Jacob first used the Hebrew term on his deathbed when he foretold the future of the 12 tribes, particularly Judah. "The scepter shall not depart from Judah, nor the ruler's staff from between his feet," the old patriarch promised, "until Shiloh comes, and to him shall be the obedience of the peoples" (Gen. 49:10). Various renderings abound, but most agree that this reference to "Shiloh" had messianic overtones, promised kings from Judah and referred to "a place of rest." Here the Tabernacle rested from its wilderness wanderings after Israel entered Canaan (see Josh. 18:1).

To me, it's more than a coincidence that the name of the place where the Tabernacle first dwelt implied the One who would ultimately fulfill its purpose. Jesus would dwell with His people. Jesus would atone for sin. Jesus would give them rest. He would *tabernacle* with us.

After lunch, the path to Shiloh's ruins led me to the outline of the Tabernacle's footprint. Climbing the crumbling rock wall required stepping over stones as large as basketballs. I moved toward what would have served as the entrance to the Tabernacle and turned about to face the courtyard. I stood in the same position as I had on the day in Timna Park when I drew back the dark curtains and entered the model alone. The size of the courtyard looked exactly the same. But this time I stood at the exact place—not just the area—where the Tabernacle had actually stood. Right here.

I made my way forward through the rubble to a small section near the back where the rocks formed a rough rectangle. After looking around and making sure of my position, I took a deep breath and pondered where I stood. If the Tabernacle sat on the footprint of these dilapidated ruins, then I was standing in the Holy of Holies. No model, no shadow, just reality . . . and chill bumps.

For three hundred years, the 12 tribes came here to Shiloh. Here Joshua parceled out the tribes' inheritance; here Hannah came to pray for a child; her son, Samuel, grew up and here the Lord revealed Himself to him (see Josh. 18; 1 Sam. 1:1-28; 3:21). But because Israel forsook God, "He abandoned the dwelling place at Shiloh, the tent which He had pitched among men, and gave up His strength to captivity and His glory into the hand of the adversary" (Ps. 78:60-61). At one time, only the high priest could stand where I stood. But now anyone—even an unbeliever—can wander around, because God has gone. Indeed, "the glory has departed" (1 Sam. 4:22). Once holiness dwelt in Shiloh, but now weeds stood as tall as my waist. Now nobody comes except a few tourists and schoolchildren who remember the glory days.

But one day God's glory would dwell with His people again—in the Temple.

—w—

This time it really *was* Elvis (or at least his statue). I couldn't believe it!

Between Tel-Aviv and Jerusalem, we pulled off Highway 1 into the parking lot of the Elvis American Diner (a.k.a. "Elvis Inn"). I exited the motor coach and looked up beneath the 16-foot-tall bronze likeness of The King. (Elvis was Jewish, I'm told.) Inside the diner, every inch of wall held pictures, postcards, LPs and all manner of Elvis memorabilia. Graceland would be proud. The music? Only Elvis, of course. Hungry? Grab an Elvis Burger or an All Shook Up Breakfast. I sat at a table next to a life-sized statue of the Big E; when Cathy pulled out the camera, I couldn't help but raise one eyebrow and curl my lip for a smile. We left with some laughs, including my favorite line: "Blue Suede Jews."

The diner reminded me of when Cathy and I ate at the Hard Rock Café in Dallas. The deafening music that night was hardly conducive to a romantic dinner ("I SAID, 'YOU LOOK LOVELY TONIGHT, SWEETHEART!' "). Built in what used to be the old McKinney Avenue Church, the Dallas café kept the building's religious look and feel. It even added a few of its own "sacred" elements, including a 50-foot-high stained-glass window of Elvis (yes, stained glass). *This is still a house of worship,* I thought.

After the men of Beth-Shemesh peeked inside the Ark of God and died, the city sent the Ark up to Kiriath-Jearim, which is, ironically, just over the hill from today's Elvis American Diner. There the Ark dwelt for about 100 years. And while it sat there ignored, the Hebrews had a request . . . a demand, really.

"Give us a king," they told Samuel, "like the other nations" (see 1 Sam. 8:5-6). God wasn't opposed to giving them a king per se. The Law of Moses had made provision for it. Jacob's promise of Shiloh even told what tribe God's chosen King would come from. But it was that last phrase—"like the other nations"—that stuck in God's craw.

29

I read somewhere that modern Israel recently hired an American magazine to photograph Jewish women in bathing suits, because—in the words of Israel's consul for media and public affairs—"We want to show that we are a normal society like all others." Those final few words leapt out to me like a déjà vu. Whether it's bikini-clad women, shopping malls, rock 'n' roll stars (The King!), or something else—Israel still seems bent on finding a way to be like all other nations.

God's glory finally moved to Jerusalem when David brought the Ark up from Kiriath-Jearim to his new capital. Later, his son Solomon built a Temple that replaced the Tabernacle. But because Israel refused to follow the Lord, God leveled Solomon's Temple like the pile of rocks that has replaced Shiloh's Tabernacle (foretold in Jer. 7:12; 26:6). Once again, the glory departed. But one day, God's glory would dwell with His people again. And this time in a *Person.*

A spry Jewish woman in her 20s led our group into a tunnel beneath a sign that read, "Western Wall Heritage." She stood before a movable scale model of the Temple Mount and demonstrated how

Herod the Great extended the base of the mount with huge retaining walls to support the elaborate expansion of the rebuilt Temple. The most famous part of this retaining wall is its western side, the Western Wall (formerly "the Wailing Wall"), which stretches 1,500 feet. Most of the wall lies underground today, accessible only through the tunnel in which we walked.

We passed a large room beneath Wilson's Arch, where Jewish men can study and pray beside the Western Wall. The area had tall ceilings, tables with chairs, and large, full bookshelves that seemed to groan under the weight of the Law.

After moving some distance north along a small hallway, with the Western Wall's massive, dressed stones to our right, we stopped about halfway down at an alcove with a single light bulb. There, an elderly Jew stood praying with a shawl on her head, her right hand on the wall and her left hand clutching a prayer book. We huddled in close.

This niche represented, the young guide explained, the closest that Jews today can get to where the Holy of Holies resided on the Temple Mount. She asserted that we stood but 300 feet from the foundation rock beneath which the Holy of Holies had stood, where God had created the world and Adam, and where Jacob had laid his head on his journey to Paddan-aram . . .

Whoa! A few biblical penalty flags went off in my head. *"Where God created the world? Where Jacob laid his head?"* Hasn't she read Genesis? But I kept quiet.

She continued. "I bring many people down here, and I try to explain holiness, and it's hard. Either you feel it or you don't."

Really? Holiness is . . . a feeling? It's always hard to explain what you don't understand. From the perspective of God's Word, holiness isn't a subjective feeling whatsoever, but an *exceedingly* objective attribute and standard: "Speak to all the congregation of the sons of Israel," God told Moses, "and say to them, 'You shall be holy, for I the LORD your God am holy'" (Lev. 19:2).

Unlike the alcove and dim bulb beneath which we stood, God "dwells in unapproachable light"—just as in the days of the Tabernacle and Temple (see 1 Tim. 6:16). Moreover, "God *is* Light"—that is, *absolute* holiness (see 1 John 1:5, emphasis added). Because God is holy, holiness remains the standard that all humanity must meet yet that all humanity—save One—has failed (see John 8:46; Rom. 3:23; Heb. 4:15).

But then again, if holiness is just a subjective feeling, so are all our ethics. And so are our facts about things like where Jacob laid his head, and how God can forgive sins—or *if* He even can.

"Destroy this temple, and in three days I will raise it up" (John 2:19). When Jesus walked on the Temple Mount, above the tunnel in which we stood, He issued this statement to the Jews to illustrate how God's glory now dwelt with people in a new way. The apostle John explained what He meant: "He was speaking of the temple of His body" (John 2:21).

In this single statement, Jesus alluded not only to the fact that God had now tabernacled with people, but also to how God would atone for sins once and for all. But they didn't get it.

Many still don't.

As the young guide stood there and spoke with all sincerity, the elderly woman continued to pray, unaffected by our presence.

—◆◆◆—

"*Shalom*," the voice on the line answered. I had called a man in Jerusalem named Dov.

"Dov?" I asked.

"*Ken.*"

"Oh, this is Ken?"

"No, this is Dov."

It took me a moment to realize Dov answered the phone in Hebrew, and *ken* means "yes." Isn't language strange?

One morning in Jerusalem, one of my Hebrew professors stood with me in the breakfast line. I thought I'd have some fun and tell him "Good morning" in Hebrew but purposely mispronounce the words.

"*Toker Bov!*"

He paused in front of the scrambled eggs and turned to me, as if disappointed. "It's *Bo . . . ker . . . Tov,*" he corrected, speaking slowly and plainly so that I could understand.

Later I discovered that even if you say it correctly, it's not necessarily conversational. I told our bus driver, "*Boker Tov,*" and he responded, "You should say, '*Boker Or*'!"—meaning "Morning light." *I give up.* God really knew what He was doing at the Tower of Babel! Languages keep us apart.

A friend told me about an energetic missionary-evangelist he saw try to communicate to a foreign audience through a dull translator. When the evangelist hollered, "Okay, folks, let's give God a hand!" the interpreter translated the words literally—and the audience blinked in confusion. *Give Him what?*

But when I went to Russia and stood before the congregation ready with the message, my interpreter stood beside me ready with the language. When my voice rose, his rose. When I gestured, so did he. After I finished each phrase, the audience's eyes darted back to Vladimir for the translation. Without him, my communication amounted to "Hello," "Goodbye," "Yes," "No" and plenty of nodding and smiling. But with Vladimir interpreting, heads nodded, eyes welled up and laughter filled the hall. He translated more than my words. He translated *me.*

I wonder if God felt a similar satisfaction when Jesus translated the message of salvation through the means of humanity. By becoming a man, Jesus put skin on God's glory and revealed the One who for centuries had remained veiled in a Temple and obscured through ritual. Jesus interpreted the Father in perfect words, actions and passions.

On the first Christmas, God gave humanity more than words— He translated Himself. He gave them One whose very words were God's Word, One whom we even call "the Word" (John 1:1).

Mary's virgin womb became the portal for God to enter the world and to fulfill Isaiah's promise of "Immanuel," which means "God with us" (Isa. 7:14; Matt. 1:23; cf. Ezek. 37:27; Zech. 2:10). Eternal God joined natures with eternal Man: "And the Word became flesh, and dwelt among us" (John 1:14). The eternal Word who was with God now was with us . . . and really, was now one of us. The glory once concealed behind the veil in the Tabernacle, God now revealed. John marveled, "And we beheld His glory" (John 1:14, *KJV*).

God had taken a major step closer to dwelling with humankind by becoming a Man. When Jesus tabernacled with us, His body became the tabernacle in which God's glory dwelt. His flesh became the veil that separated God's holiness from man's sinfulness. He became the one entrance to God. He became the final priest and mediator. He became the atoning sacrifice through His death on the cross. And His resurrection proved that God was satisfied with it all (see Rom. 3:25; 4:25; 1 Tim. 2:5-6; Heb. 7:24-25). He even maintains an intercessory role for believers today.

And yet, to those who knew Him, Jesus seemed as displaced as Elvis does in Israel today—odd, incompatible, almost profane. Jesus didn't fit their expectations of a king "like all the nations."

Even the wise magi didn't come first to Bethlehem to look for Jesus. They headed to Jerusalem, to the place where kings were supposed to live. Jesus' own family thought He was crazy. And the religious leaders? They blamed Satan. Jesus disappointed most everybody.

Even those who walked in the footsteps of Jesus up and down the Holy Land—those He chose as His disciples—even *they* stumbled over their expectations of who He should be.

We all do.

CHAPTER TWO

GREAT EXPECTATIONS AND
TEMPTATIONS

*"Rabbi, we know that You have come from God as a teacher;
for no one can do these signs that You do unless God is with him."*
JOHN 3:2

I made my way to the Western Wall early that morning.

As I opened my bag for the military security inside Jerusalem's Dung Gate, I noticed that ultra-orthodox Jews could walk right through the metal detector without stopping. They were headed the same direction as me.

The wall—called Kotel in Hebrew—towers 50 feet above the people below and shaded the busy goings-on from the morning sun. Branches of wild caper and hyssop grew out of the cracks in the wall, bespeaking the fill dirt behind it that Herod the Great brought in to expand the Temple Mount above. The stones pinched in their gaps countless scraps of paper on which people had scrawled their prayers. (Prayers are removed once a year.)

As I waited for the ceremonies to begin, I studied the assortment of people. Many of the orthodox Jewish men looked like Westerners apart from their yarmulkes, or skullcaps, held fast by hairpins. The ultra-orthodox wear the traditional black garb, even in the heat of summer. I spied one elderly ultra-orthodox man approaching the wall. The gentle soul couldn't have been four-and-a-half feet tall. Shuffling with the aid of a walker, toes turned out, each step advanced him only inches. He finally reached up to touch where millions of Jewish hands have stained the wall six feet high in the last half century.

On the other side of the compound, younger orthodox Jews smoked cigarettes, chatted and laughed together. Another Jew read a prayer book and sat alongside a soldier chewing his nails. A laugh, a cry, a sneeze—all sound the same in any language. The area looked clean, bright and pleasant. Crowds began to fill the empty spaces. A single Israeli flag flapped above us. I thought, *I love coming here.*

Every sort of seat—from plastic lawn chairs and metal folding chairs to wooden stools and benches—sat arrayed in the open area facing the ancient stones. Old women and young mothers with shawls and cameras watched behind a concrete partition. Below them, groups of men and boys surrounded tables covered with scrolls and bright blue cloth. Then it began.

I observed a 13-year-old boy and his father standing among their male relatives. The boy wore *tefillin* (phylacteries, which are small boxes that contain scrolls of biblical parchment) on his forehead and arms, a white embroidered *tallit* (prayer shawl) over his head, arm-bands and wire-rimmed glasses—a sharp-looking kid. His father had donned a simple yarmulke, sunglasses and a wide smile. The father showed his son how to perform certain motions like touching his head, raising and lowering his hand in a rhythmic manner, kissing the scrolls and his fingers, and reciting prayers from a yellow slip of paper.

While the father and son exchanged motions, others around the table filled the space with song. One of these men, a portly man who I'd guess was in his 60s, served as the *chazzan* (cantor) and sang with absolute abandon, his lungs full. His voice was terrible, but because of passion, also beautiful. A child in the distance played a drum but stopped abruptly when his mother rebuked him and took it away. *People are just people everywhere,* I smiled. *Well . . . almost.*

Just then, the women behind the partition emitted a howl like the war cries of American Indians in the movies. I'm serious—*just* like Indians. I looked around, but no one else seemed concerned. The father continued each motion for his son with meticulous precision, and when the ceremony concluded, the daddy beamed with pride. His boy was now a man.

The ritual called a *bar mitzvah* represents a Jewish male's transition from childhood to adulthood. As a "son of the Law," the young man now had the responsibility to fulfill the Mosaic Law—and received a certificate that said so.

Talk about an impossible task!

As I watched the goings-on with curious delight, I thought about another Jewish boy, about the same age, who came to Jerusalem many years earlier. But instead of coming to the Kotel, the boy went onto the Temple Mount itself above and behind the wall. When the time came to head home, the boy Jesus stayed behind in Jerusalem—and it took Joseph and Mary three days to find Him (see Luke 2:41-50).

Can you imagine their angst? God has entrusted *you* with the monumental task of raising the Son of God, the Messiah—*and you lost Him!*

"Why is it that you were looking for Me?" Jesus asked His fretful parents when they finally found Him in the Temple. "Did you not know that I had to be in My Father's house?" (Luke 2:49). No, they didn't know that. Luke says they didn't even comprehend this statement. I'm not sure I do either.

So began a long list of people misunderstanding Jesus.

Every year His family had gone to Jerusalem for the Passover. Every year Jesus had returned with them. But this year He had stayed behind and told no one. We should note that just because people misunderstood Him—even His parents—that doesn't mean Jesus did anything wrong. "He *continued* in subjection to them," Luke tells us (Luke 2:51, emphasis added). That means He never stopped being obedient, even when He confused everyone by staying behind.

Some scholars say Jesus' Passover visit to Jerusalem at age 12 represented His bar mitzvah, or its equivalent, even though the modern ceremony I witnessed may not have existed in Jesus' day. Maybe so. But however you look at it, Jesus clearly understood Himself as the Son of God from an early age. He understood that His purpose had to do with the work of the Father. He had an extraordinary wisdom. Jesus was indeed a "son of the Law."

Because Scripture says very little about Jesus' early years, a few self-appointed prophets have inspired some stories of their own. Read them when you need a good laugh. My favorite excerpts come from the *Infancy Story of Thomas*, where we read that one day, the boy

Jesus was working in the woodshop with Joseph. Joseph needed two equal boards but one measured too short. So Jesus took hold of the board and stretched it![1] As a woodworker myself, I would love to have Jesus around the shop.

Just don't make Him mad. More than once in the fanciful fiction, Jesus gets irate at His playmates and they fall over dead.[2] Sounds like a trailer for a Stephen King movie, doesn't it? "How would you like *YOUR* children to play with Jesus?" Good grief. Is this the same Jesus who later invited, "Let the little children come to me" (Luke 18:16, *NIV*)? Methinks not.

Between the Passover when He was 12 and the next 18-plus years before He began His ministry, Scripture gives us only one verse that refers to Jesus' upbringing in Nazareth (see Luke 2:52). One verse! Wouldn't it be nice to have seen a perfect toddler? Or teenager? Or adult single man?

In a way, Scripture *isn't* silent on what Jesus did all that time. He did much more than build tables and chairs. What the Bible records next tells us so.

37

—✤—

Far in the north, the melting snows of Mount Hermon seep underground and resurface at Caesarea Philippi and Dan, forming the headwaters of the Jordan River. "Jordan" comes from the Hebrew term *yarad*, meaning "to go down, to descend." As the fresh water runs southward, down through the Jordan Rift Valley, it empties into the northern end of the Sea of Galilee. The river resumes its journey at the southern end of the Sea of Galilee, snaking through white-barked, birch-like trees that canopy the whole river with shade. The sun occasionally pierces the branches where birds take wing and twitter.

A sidewalk led to a short, stepped, concrete ramp along the Jordan's western bank. Here stood a sign with lettering etched in framed glass. I walked up to read it: "Close to where Jesus was baptised." *Hmm.* I saw another sign, in Hebrew and English, beside the steep banks of the river itself: "Going down to the water is forbidden."

Exploring the Judean Wilderness where Jesus was tempted.

Teaching about the life of Jesus from the Nazareth Ridge
in Galilee, overlooking the Jezreel Valley.

Ahead, concrete walkways dipped into the Jordan's gentle current at several spots, and handrails stood ready to keep surefooted those who entered the water. The Yardenit baptismal facility rents white robes to those who want to be baptized, but some folks wade in without them. Watching the people in the river, I witnessed almost every mode of baptism in church tradition. One grandmother from India entered fully clothed and had her daughter dip a plastic pitcher into the river and repeatedly empty it over her head until the old woman was drenched.

In another area, pastors baptized their congregants while little fish in the river nipped at the hairs on the pastors' legs: "I baptize you in the . . . ouch! . . . in the name of the Father and of the . . . ouch!" As people returned their rented robes, he or she received a framable certificate certifying their baptism in the Jordan River.

The path to the exit funneled everyone through a large, climate-controlled gift shop (standard procedure for most stops) that sold books, Bibles, calendars, olive wood, olive oil, film and very expensive rugs. Air-conditioning was free.

As our bus departed and followed the southerly path of the Jordan River, we descended a mere 60 miles to 1,300 feet below sea level. Interestingly, the Jordan River covers this same distance by snaking and winding back and forth over 125 miles before it empties into the Dead Sea below Jericho. Today, domestic and agricultural interests have diverted about 90 percent of the Jordan's flow—with sewage replacing it. For this reason, in June 2007, the World Monuments Fund designated the Jordan River an Endangered Cultural Heritage Site.[3]

This part of the Jordan River—too hot, too political and hardly picturesque—draws fewer tourists than up north. But it should attract thousands. Because here above the Dead Sea, across from Jericho, near what the Bible calls "Bethany beyond the Jordan," John baptized Jesus Christ in the Jordan River (John 1:28).[4]

When we picture John the Baptist, we usually imagine a hairy, half-crazed wild-man, standing knee-deep in the river and screaming with a pointed finger: "Repent!" John's message to Israel had its roots in a principle given just across the Jordan on its eastern side.

Camped on the Plains of Moab, Moses wrote the book of Deuteronomy to describe the requirement of Israel's obedience before God would bring blessings (see Deut. 28:1-14). The Greek term for "repent" literally means "a change of mind." We get the cart before the horse when we think that "repent" simply means to change one's actions. No lasting change comes until the mind changes first (see Rom. 12:1-2).

The Law revealed sin, and John called people to admit their sin and repent so that blessing would come—the blessing of "the kingdom of heaven" (see 2 Chron. 7:14; Matt. 3:2; Rom. 7:7; 1 Cor. 15:56; Gal. 3:24). Israel understood that the kingdom the prophets promised would be the age when the Messiah, the son of David, would reign over the world from Jerusalem and usher in God's blessings (see 2 Sam. 7:16; Ps. 2; Isa. 9:6-7; Jer. 33:15).

Yet to go out to John at the Jordan, as all Judea did, implied a break with the current system—or at least a transition from it. As the son of a priest, John should have carried out his ministry as a priest in the Temple. But instead, John screamed as a prophet in the wilderness. Rather than enjoy the choice food of a priest, John crunched locusts with wild honey. Rather than wear fine priestly linen, John donned camel's hair and a leather belt, reminiscent of Elijah (see 2 Kings 1:8; Mark 1:6). John even baptized in the same area of the Jordan where Elijah ascended to heaven in a chariot of fire (see 2 Kings 2:11).

But John was no rebel. The odd elements of his ministry—his words, his wardrobe and his whereabouts—served as clues to reveal that John represented the "Elijah messenger," who would point to the Messiah (see Mal. 3:1; 4:5). Anyone can baptize with water, but only the Messiah, John went on, "will baptize you with the Holy Spirit" (Mark 1:8; see also Matt. 3:11; Luke 3:16).

John pointed to Jesus as "the Lamb of God who takes away the sin of the world!" (John 1:29). At Passover each year, lambs were sacrificed to commemorate Israel's redemption from bondage in Egypt. Describing Jesus as God's Lamb pointed to the fact that Jesus would die as a substitute. Taking "away the sin of the world" meant that Jesus would replace the Old Covenant of Law with the predicted New Covenant, which promised forgiveness of sins (see Jer. 31:31-34).

Putting it together, John's message becomes concise: To enter God's kingdom, admit that you are a sinner and turn to Jesus, who will remove your sins through His death on your behalf. Billy Graham could have preached it no clearer.

But notice a seeming contradiction in John's message: Jesus will reign over God's eternal kingdom; Jesus will die for the sins of the world. See the problem? How can the Messiah reign if He's dead? Prior to Jesus' resurrection, no one understood this dilemma. Everyone clutched the promises of the Messiah's kingdom blessings and swept the "dying Messiah" part under the rug. Even John did. And it would come as a hard lesson.

Jesus knew that before the blessings of the Kingdom could come, the problem of sin had to be dealt with—not simply *confession* of sin, but *remission* of sin. Not by mere baptism in the Jordan, but by a "baptism" Jesus would endure later—on the cross (see Mark 10:38; Luke 12:50). Jesus' water baptism that day began the long road to His other "baptism"—His crucifixion.

After Jesus' baptism in the Jordan, He saw the heavens opening— literally, "tearing"—and the Holy Spirit descending amidst the Father's accolades: "You are My beloved Son, in You I am well-pleased" (Mark 1:11). Even the tearing open of heaven suggested a transition to a new era. Something simply "opened" could conceivably be closed again. But what's torn *stays* torn—that is, it stays open. Mark's only other use of the Greek term for "tear" makes this point powerfully clear (see Mark 15:38): God was opening a way to heaven through His Son. Isaiah's ancient plea, "Oh, that You would rend the heavens and come down," had begun to come true (Isa. 64:1).

The Father's approval of the Son also revealed that Jesus' baptism had nothing to do with personal repentance from sin. Baptism, in its most basic sense, represents *identification with* someone or something—a metaphorical use the New Testament often employs (see Luke 12:50; Rom. 6:3; 1 Cor. 10:2; 12:13; 1 Pet. 3:21). Water baptism simply signifies identification. Jesus *identified with* sinners in His baptism—and then also, immediately thereafter, in His temptation to become a sinner. I'm glad all baptisms aren't followed by the level of temptation Jesus endured.

I have walked in the wilderness where Satan tempted Christ, just west of where He was baptized. Good grief, what a place. This is the wilderness of Judea where God shaped the character of the future King David in "the valley of the shadow of death" (Ps. 23:4). Here David prayed, "My flesh yearns for You, in a dry and weary land where there is no water" (Ps. 63:1). David wasn't kidding. Endless piles of rocks, steep hills, no trees, meager vegetation, little water, slight shade and lizards. As far as my eye could see, it was empty, dry and depressing. I tried to imagine the solitude and struggle Jesus would have endured here for over a month. But I could not.

We can barely stand to fast for a day or two. Can you imagine fasting 40 days? Jesus did so in preparation for temptation—and became *desperately* hungry and needy. And in His moment of need, the devil slipped in. (Satan waits for moments like these.)

"If You are the Son of God, tell this stone to become bread" (Luke 4:3).

The devil is no idiot—and also no gentleman. When he tempts, he plays dirty. No rules. No concessions. No mercy. He waited for a moment of vulnerability and then tempted Jesus to satisfy His legitimate need for food in an illegitimate way: "Turn this stone to bread—use your power to gratify your need." What a cheap shot. *Every* stone would then become a temptation. And believe me, the wilderness of Judea has plenty of stones! Jesus' reply shows that—though He was physically hungry—He was spiritually full.

"It is written, 'Man shall not live on bread alone'" (Luke 4:4).

In Israel, few tourists live on bread alone. At one buffet in Eilat, I stood agape at the options: bagels, buns, nuts, jellies, raw fish, red and green apples, grapes, peaches, pears, melons, apricots, nectarines, salads, pastries, flan (I call it "phlegm") and chocolate cheesecakes—all surrounded by an assortment of fresh fruit juices. And this was just breakfast. Each meal looked like an advertisement for a five-star restaurant. So yes, we ate well—like kings, usually.

But on my longest trip, I studied in Israel for several weeks and stayed in a cheap Jerusalem hotel in the Old City. The place served the same thing for breakfast every morning. After eight days of wet scrambled eggs, I felt like I was gathering manna in the wilderness . . . that or growing feathers.

What had Jesus, the meek and mild carpenter, been doing all those silent years growing up in Nazareth?

We just saw it. His first words reveal it to us.

"It is written."

Jesus grew up with a hammer in one hand and a scroll in the other. He prepared for three-and-a-half years of ministry by spending about three-and-a-half decades learning the Word of God. And He learned it by living it; hence, the Father's commendation at Jesus' baptism.

Jesus quoted from Deuteronomy, the book written just across the river. Here Moses had reminded Israel that God led them into the wilderness to humble them and to test them for 40 years—just like the Spirit led Jesus in the wilderness for 40 days. God allowed the Hebrews to hunger and then fed them with manna to teach them "that man does not live by bread alone, but man lives by everything that proceeds out of the mouth of the LORD" (Deut. 8:3). Even gathering manna had rules.

The Son of God had the power to meet His need in an illegitimate way—but He refused. And by His being "tempted in all things as we are," He gained experience that allows Him to serve as a sympathetic High Priest to our weaknesses (Heb. 4:15; see also Heb. 2:18; 4:14-16).

Jesus had become a "son of the Law"—a bar mitzvah—in the truest sense.

—⁓—

Our guide pointed from the road to a rocky outcropping on one of the distant hills.

"This hike is definitely optional," he warned us. "But it's worth it."

A few of us brave souls followed, and for the first time in my life, I wished I had four legs. The quarter-mile climb between the bus and that outcrop proved the hardest hike I took in Israel. The loose rocks over which I toddled were large, hot and pokey. I had to calculate every step. There was no enjoying the view. Our guide scurried over the rocks like a lizard and stopped ahead, halfway up the hill, near the fissure in the rocks to which he had pointed. He turned and stood, arms crossed, one leg over the other, and waited for us. Finally I arrived.

"This is it," he beamed.

Still panting, I entered the small cave, which inside looked about the size of a tiny bedroom. Empty . . . but bursting with significance. The contrast between the crudity of the cave and the profundity of its history still staggers me.

In 1947, a Bedouin shepherd allegedly lost a sheep and tossed a rock in this cave to search for the animal. Why—or *how*—a sheep would ever wander up here makes no sense. Our guide told us the Bedouin more likely was a looter in sheep's clothing who fabricated the whole affair to legitimize his discovery. Anyhow, what he found in the cave made biblical history—or rather, I should say, confirmed it.

45

I turned and looked back out the cave at the Dead Sea below me. In this area just southeast of where Jesus was tempted—and during the same century—a small community at Qumran scribbled copies of the Old Testament and other literature. They sealed their scrolls in clay jars and hid them in caves near the shores of the Dead Sea—the place from which these now famous scrolls received their name. I stood in "Cave 1," so called because it was found first.

Prior to the discovery of the Dead Sea Scrolls, scholars despaired of ever finding Hebrew manuscripts that predated our oldest copies, which were from the tenth century A.D. But the finds at Qumran dated from the second century B.C.—and backed up our understanding of the Hebrew Bible by about *one thousand years!* Eleven caves at Qumran have produced copies of every Old Testament book except Esther, verifying that the copies we had were accurate and reliable all along. The Old Testament we read today is the same as Jesus read, only translated.

In a book published not long before the discovery, Frederic G. Kenyon wrote despairingly, "There is, indeed, no probability that we shall ever find manuscripts of the Hebrew text going back to a period before the formation of the text which we know as Massoretic. We can only arrive at an idea of it by a study of the earliest translations made from it."[5] Only eight years later, the Dead Sea Scrolls were discovered.

Isn't this often how we view life? Utterly hopeless, and then God steps in. Any one of us could have written something similar to Kenyon's quote. Situations and conditions often seem hopeless— *most* often, actually. Outcomes and attitudes will appear unchangeable and literally demand we doubt God's Word.

But circumstances have nothing to do with trust—Adam's fall in Eden proves that. Even paradise had its temptations! The same areas of temptation to which Adam yielded, Jesus, the Last Adam, faced and conquered (compare Gen. 3:1-6 with Luke 4:1-13).

The devil challenges us to "repent" too—to change our minds about God's Word. Every temptation we fail represents a repentance in the wrong direction. Satan's tactics of disguising the truth and deceiving mankind haven't changed since Eden (see 2 Cor. 4:4; 11:3,14; 1 John 2:16). Nor has God changed the means of victory over temptation: trust and obedience to His Word (see Ps. 119:9-11; Col. 2:8).

Adam's failure and Christ's success swung on the same hinge—a response to God's Word. Both knew God's commands. Both endured Satan's temptation to doubt them. But only one trusted God's Word over the circumstances.

In another temptation, Satan took Jesus to a "high mountain" and offered Him all the kingdoms of the world in exchange for worship (Matt. 4:8; see also Luke 4:5-7). Jesus knew the Father had promised that His Son would rule the world—but only after the suffering of the cross (see Ps. 2; Luke 24:26). Satan offered Jesus the fast track to glory by skipping the suffering (and it wouldn't be the last time Satan does this). Jesus' response? "It is written, 'You shall worship the Lord your God and serve Him only' " (Luke 4:8; cf. Matt. 4:10). Another point for Jesus.

Satan also took Jesus to Jerusalem, to the pinnacle of the Temple, and by misapplying Scripture, tempted Him to jump off and let God save Him. Jesus' reaction? In all three temptations Jesus responded with Scripture—from the book of Deuteronomy (see Luke 4:4-12; see also Matt. 4:4-10). Jesus didn't say, "Okay now, wait a minute, where's My concordance?" Jesus knew the Word and clung to it. How would you like to go toe to toe with temptation, relying only on your memory of the book of Deuteronomy?

I grew up seeing the Bible as my Sunday ornament. I had my tie, my coat, my dress shoes and a book. The Word of God played no more a role in my life than the clip-on tie I wore for an hour on Sundays. I remember my genuine surprise in my early 20s when I discovered that this book communicated not just words on a page, but the words of life—*my life*. I still marvel that the Creator has preserved His truth for millennia so that I may know and do His will. What a gift.

In Jerusalem today stands the Shrine of the Book, a museum that displays the Dead Sea Scrolls. I've been there a number of times. The shrine's massive white roof, shaped like the lid of one of the clay jars the scrolls were found in, stands opposite a large black wall of granite. The contrasting colors represent the "sons of light" and the "sons of darkness" and imply a principle: God's Word represents the difference between light and darkness (see Ps. 119:105; 2 Pet. 1:19).

God verifies the reliability of Scripture by many means, including resurrecting ancient manuscripts from the caves of Qumran and raising His Son from the cave that was His tomb. But the task of living His Word, God gives as our responsibility: "Every word of God is tested; He is a shield to those who take refuge in Him" (Prov. 30:5).

Jesus revealed that to walk in the light takes more than having God's Word; it takes belief and obedience to the Word—even when the darkest of times tempts us to doubt. And they will.

—∽∾—

After spending some time in Galilee, where He turned water into wine and called a few fishermen to follow Him, Jesus journeyed to Jerusalem for the first Passover of His ministry. There He cleansed the Temple, taught the people and performed miraculous signs (see John 2). One night, Jesus received a visitor from the Jewish religious council.

"Rabbi, we know that You have come from God as a teacher," Nicodemus began, "for no one can do these signs that You do unless God is with him" (John 3:2).

"A teacher." Is that all? Jesus wanted him to see more. So the Savior revealed a need in Nicodemus's heart.

"Unless one is born again," Jesus explained, "he cannot see the kingdom of God" (John 3:3). But Nicodemus misinterpreted the statement as physical birth. So Jesus explained "born again" as a spiritual event. The Pharisee still didn't get it.

"Are you the teacher of Israel and do not understand these things?" (John 3:10). With that question, I bet Nicodemus felt like a little boy on the Temple steps, struggling to learn his Hebrew alphabet. He *should* have known what "born again" meant. For the first time in years, Israel's teacher was stumped.

Jesus' famous phrase "born again" probably alluded to the short, enigmatic Psalm 87. Here God spoke of those who were physically born on foreign soil as spiritually born in Zion—in Jerusalem.[6] "The LORD will write in the register of the peoples: 'This one was born in Zion'" (Ps. 87:6, *NIV*). Jesus told Nicodemus that getting into God's kingdom requires a spiritual rebirth.

That was the need—*spiritual life*. And it came about through faith in God's Son, who would be lifted up like the serpent Moses lifted up in the wilderness (see John 3:14-16; see also Num. 21:7-9).

I entered the church mostly out of curiosity. It stood as the only building on top of the mountain. The inside looked like a combination chapel and archaeological dig. Mosaics and rugs checkerboarded the floor. Below the roof of unpainted I-beams and skylights, a single flute began a melody while a cluster of Germans on simple benches sang a hymn I'd never heard. Up front, two white-robed priests with palms together stood before a limestone altar. Behind them a large semicircle of stacked stones sat beneath three stained-glass windows. The center window depicted Moses lifting up the serpent in the wilderness.

I exited the Church of St. George and walked to the edge of the cliff that overlooked the Jordan Rift Valley. I stood on Pisgah, also called Mount Nebo, where the prophet Balaam overlooked the Hebrews camped on the Plains of Moab below (see Num. 23:14). In this vast flatland before the Jordan River, Moses penned the book of Deuteronomy to a people prepared to enter a land they had waited 40 years to acquire. I tried to picture the millions of Hebrews camped at the base of the hills. I imagined their anticipation (especially the ladies) of leaving behind their tents and finally having homes to dwell in. The Hebrew word for "tent" is *ohel*, pronounced (and I'm not kidding) "Oh, hell"—a sentiment that has nothing to do with the original word but probably had a lot to do with how the Hebrews felt, having lived in the wilderness for 40 years!

According to the end of Deuteronomy, God told Moses to stand atop the hill where I stood and take his first and final view of the Promised Land. I can't imagine his disappointment at having come so far so long and then not being allowed to enter the land because of his outburst of anger—his dishonoring God "in the midst of the sons of Israel" (Deut. 32:51; see also Deut. 32:50-52; 34:1). As I stare again in my mind's eye, I think long on the necessity of my own faithfulness and integrity as a leader—whether in my home, work or ministry. If God removed the humble Moses' privilege of service—even his life!—how much more tenuous is mine? Moses' final speech to the Hebrews, and to all of us, came from the trembling voice of experience: "For it is not an idle word for you; indeed it is your life. And by this word you will prolong your days in the land, which you are about to cross the Jordan to possess" (Deut. 32:47).

To my right stood a rusty wrought-iron statue of a snake coiling a tall pole. It reminded me of the Staff of Asclepius, the symbol of modern medicine. The figure clearly depicted the serpent that Moses lifted up in the wilderness. But this statue on Nebo had a pole shaped differently, unusually—like a cross. It instantly connected me to Jesus' statement about how to be born again: "As Moses lifted up the serpent in the wilderness, even so must the Son of Man be lifted up; so that whoever believes will in Him have eternal life" (John 3:14-15).

God told Moses to set a bronze serpent up on a standard so that those Hebrews who had been bitten by fiery snakes could look at it and be healed; a look of faith removed the lethal effects of the poison (see Num. 21:7-9). Jesus used this to illustrate the means by which God would remove the effects of sin from the life of anyone who looks to Him in faith.

Jesus would be lifted up on the cross "so that whoever believes in Him will have eternal life" (John 3:15).

—⁂—

"Why can't I just pray to God without Jesus in the middle?"

A Jewish friend of mine in Israel asked this question. Amir's life, by his own admission, had no hope; he had even considered ending it. The lady he spoke to, a messianic Jew, answered his question.

"Why don't you just pray that God will reveal to you who Jesus is all about?" So for the first time, Amir sat down, wrote out a prayer, stuck it on the wall where he could see it and prayed.

"And I made sure I said every word."

Amir opened the morning newspaper and, mortified, immediately slammed it shut. He slowly opened it again, and what he saw was still there. "*YESHUA*," Jesus' name in Hebrew, stood out in large letters on the page. Campus Crusade for Christ planned to show the *Jesus* film that night in Jerusalem.

"I watched the movie and knew all those Old Testament prophecies," Amir related. "I could see them being fulfilled. At the end of the movie, it was either I accept it or reject it—but I cannot stay apathetic." The Jewish authorities afterward realized the purpose of the movie—that it offered people the chance to accept Jesus as the Messiah—and they promptly removed the movie after one night.

"But that was the night that the Lord designed for me," Amir declared. "I decided to accept it, because it was clear to me that this is the truth." And of all places—remember this was Israel, with the Jordan River and everything—Amir was baptized in a swimming pool. Three days later, he began his service in the Israeli Defense Force.

After Amir became an officer, the army asked where he would like them to station him. "Give me the most boring place in this country," Amir requested.

"Why don't you go to Jericho? No one wants to go there." So he went.

Two weeks later, Jericho became the eye of a political storm and the first city that Israel handed over to Palestinian control—with Amir himself handing over the keys of the city. He served as deputy-governor, second in command, in charge of 300 soldiers and 17,000 civilians.

"God has a sense of humor," Amir smiled. Today Amir serves as one of the most sought-after tour guides in Israel.

As I stood atop Mount Nebo beside the rusting statue of the serpent coiling a cross, I scanned the Jericho valley where Amir had served. I could see the Jordan River where Jesus was baptized. Beyond it lay the Judean Wilderness, where Jesus stood firm in temptation by quoting the Scriptures Moses penned on the plains below me. I could see the Dead Sea to the south, next to Qumran, where the Scriptures were preserved for 2,000 years. Through the haze in the far distance I could see what Moses saw on the day he stood here. The distant horizon traced the ridge of the Mount of Olives, behind which sat Jerusalem, where the symbol of the wrought-iron cross next to me found its fulfillment.

After the talk with Nicodemus, Jesus spent the rest of the summer and fall of A.D. 30 in Jerusalem and Judea. But when He heard of John the Baptist's arrest and imprisonment, Jesus departed for Galilee again.

Before our group left Jerusalem for Galilee, I went again to the Western Wall. Amidst the usual hubbub of prayers and chanting, I saw a tall American tourist with his head covered and bowed, praying with both hands on the wall. He was older, probably retired, with white legs and bright clothes, and stood beside a line of rocking Jews. When he finished, I questioned him about his prayer.

He told me he had prayed for a Jewish man back in the States who had yet to trust Christ. He wanted to be able to tell the man that he had prayed for him at the Western Wall. Later that year I followed up with the gentleman, named Les, and asked about the Jew he had prayed for.

"He passed away," Les told me. He paused and then added, "Probably without Christ."

"Unless one is born again," Jesus told Nicodemus, "he cannot see the kingdom of God."

It was dark when the Pharisee first came to Jesus—as dark as the black granite wall that stands opposite the Shrine of the Book today. "The Light has come into the world," Jesus told him, "and men loved the darkness rather than the Light, for their deeds were evil" (John 3:19). At some point though, the Light entered Nicodemus's heart. He became born again, for he would believe in Jesus as the Savior the Old Testament had promised (see John 19:39).

Just like Amir did.

Notes

1. Wilhelm Schneemelcher, ed., *New Testament Apocrypha,* vol. 1, English translation ed. R. McL. Wilson, rev. ed. (Louisville, KY: Westminster/John Knox Press, 1991), pp. 439-453.
2. Ibid.
3. Michele Chabin, RNS, with reporting by Elizabeth Lawson, "Weeping for the Jordan," *Christianity Today,* vol. 51, no. 9 (September 2007), p. 17.
4. J. Carl Laney, *Selective Geographical Problems in the Life of Christ* (dissertation, Dallas Theological Seminary, 1977), pp. 50-70.
5. Frederic G. Kenyon, *Our Bible and the Ancient Manuscripts: Being a History of the Texts and Its Translations,* 4th ed. (London, England: Eyre and Spottiswoode, 1939), p. 48.
6. Ron B. Allen, "A Song Seldom Sung" (message, Stonebriar Community Church, Frisco, TX, August 5, 2007). It was Dr. Allen who had the insight to connect John 3 to Psalm 87.

CHAPTER THREE

DISAPPOINTED WITH PERFECTION

When John, while imprisoned, heard of the works of Christ,
he sent word by his disciples and said to Him,
"Are You the Expected One, or shall we look for someone else?"

MATTHEW 11:2-3

When Jesus left Judea for Galilee, the book of John tells us, "He had to pass through Samaria" (John 4:4).

No, He didn't.

At least, not *geographically*.

The ancient road Jesus walked from Judea to Galilee led through Samaria, true. But Jesus could have taken another route from Jerusalem—down to Jericho and north through the Jordan Rift Valley toward Galilee. In fact, many Jews preferred this longer, warmer route during the winter months. And this way also afforded them another benefit—they avoided the Samaritans.

After the Northern Kingdom of Israel went into exile in 722 B.C., the Assyrians' repopulation of the area between Galilee and Judea produced a mixed race—part Jewish, part Gentile. The region took on the name "Samaria" after the former capital city of the Northern Kingdom. When the Jews returned from exile, these Samaritan half-breeds asked to help rebuild the Temple in Jerusalem. Zerubbabel, the governor of Judah, flatly refused them (see Ezra 4:2-3).

So the Samaritans developed their own religion—based on the Pentateuch alone, excluding the rest of the Hebrew Scriptures—and built their own rival temple on Mount Gerizim, next to Shechem (see 2 Kings 17:24-41). In 129 B.C., John Hyrcanus, a leader of the Jews, widened the rift between the Jews and Samaritans by destroying the Samaritans' temple. By the time Jesus headed through Samaria, the racial hatred between the Jews and Samaritans stood at fever pitch. Today, only a few hundred Samaritans exist in the Holy Land, but they still worship and sacrifice on Mount Gerizim.

I like the way the old *King James Version* renders the English of John 4:4: "He must needs go through Samaria." Jesus' need to travel that way was not geographical—but *spiritual*.

Our bus rumbled north along the same path Jesus walked, part of which has become a four-lane highway. This ancient road, called the "Way of the Patriarchs," received its name from the heroes of Genesis who traveled north and south along this watershed of the Hill Country. The road stretches from Beersheba in the south, north through Hebron, Bethlehem, Jerusalem, Ramah, Bethel, Gibeah and finally Shechem, where Abraham first came when he entered the land of Canaan (see Gen. 12:5-7).

Here God promised Abraham (then Abram) that He would give his descendants this land, later confirming His covenant with Abraham's son Isaac, not Ishmael (see Gen. 17:18-21; 21:10; 26:4). That means that God promised the land to the Jews, not to the Arabian descendants of Ishmael—representing most Palestinians in modern Israel. But God *did* make provision for the foreigner to live in the land alongside the Hebrews, a fact many people overlook today (see Num. 9:14; Deut. 14:29). But this provision, of course, does not require a tolerance for terrorism.

The city of Nablus lies about a mile northwest of Old Testament Shechem. Founded in A.D. 72 as Neapolis ("New City"), the city's name has changed to Nablus to reflect an Arabic pronunciation, but Jews still call it Shechem. Ironically, in Nablus/Shechem—where God promised the land to Abraham—today there remains one of the most volatile Palestinian hot spots in the West Bank. You'll often hear the name of the city in the news. In fact, of the string of cities I mentioned that dot the Way of the Patriarchs, only Jerusalem offers Jews a welcome mat. All others, excluding Beersheba and including Bethlehem, are Palestinian cities. Even tourists should visit only when the political climate allows—an unfortunate rarity.

Our motor coach slowed before a road sign: "Prepare documents for inspection." The checkpoint made clear that we were entering Palestinian territory. *Smiles, everyone! Smiles!*

On the outskirts of Nablus, we parallel parked in the street with the bus honking rhythmically as it backed up. Once we disembarked, we stood before an unassuming, gated compound with a hand-painted sign that read "Greek Orthodox Convent," with something scrawled below in Arabic. Through the gate and down some steps we found ourselves inside a half-built church with scaffolding, high stone walls, and sky for ceiling. At the back by the altar stood what looked like two tall, whitewashed wooden doghouses. We entered the doghouses to discover a medieval stairwell with little headroom, leading underground. We descended to a T-shaped crypt like a basement, small and dim. There, rising from the floor before us stood the purpose of our stop.

A well.

On His journey north from Judea to Galilee, a weary Jesus rested by this well while His disciples went into the city of Sychar for some fast food. The Crusaders identified Sychar as the Greek form of Shechem, but others identify it with Askar, just north of the well along the eastern slope of Mount Ebal. And the identification of the well itself? Jacob's Well remains one of the few sites in Israel no one disputes. That's significant, especially because the well has survived since the time Jacob willed it to Joseph in 1859 B.C.—*well* over 3,800 years ago! (Pun intended.)

Jesus would have journeyed this way many, many times as a boy traveling with His family to and from Jerusalem for the Passover. Most certainly, they paused at the well for refreshment. Joseph and Mary would have instructed their children as they walked "by the way" (Deut. 6:7), rehearsing the momentous events that occurred in Shechem. As Jesus rested alone by the well, waiting for His disciples' return, He could have glanced up from the valley in which He sat and seen the two mountains towering on either side of Him. His parents' nostalgic lessons would have come easily to mind.

After Moses brought the Hebrews out of Egypt, God commanded Israel to enter the Promised Land and come here to Shechem to shout the promised blessings and curses of the Mosaic Covenant (see Deut. 27–28). Joshua did so, with half of the people standing on

Mount Ebal to shout the curses that would come for disobedience, and half standing on Mount Gerizim to shout the blessings that would come for obedience. Joshua would later gather the people again to Shechem, reminding them of their previous pledge (see Josh. 8:30-35; 24). Joshua also designated Shechem as one of the three cities of refuge on the west side of the Jordan (see Josh. 20:7; 21:21; 1 Chron. 6:67).

God's blessings and curses flowed primarily from a simple element of nature: water. Because the land of Israel lacked a natural abundance of water, the Hebrews depended on rain for life—and rainfall depended on their obedience to God. Rain represented God's literal blessing on the earth, and the lack of rain, God's curse (Deut. 28:12, 23-24; Pss. 65:9-13; 72:6-7; 107:33-38; Mic. 5:7). "Living water" represented a fresh, moving source, like a spring, an image Jeremiah compared to a direct relationship with the Lord (see Jer. 2:13).

Suddenly, all Jesus' nostalgia stopped. Soft footsteps approached.

About high noon, He turned to see a water jar on the head of a lone woman—a Samaritan. Surprised, she stared awkwardly. Then Jesus did the unthinkable. He spoke to her.

"Give Me a drink" (John 4:7).

With those four words (only three in Greek), Jesus crossed major cultural barriers. John reminds us: "Jews have no dealings with Samaritans" (John 4:9). She then asked Jesus—a male, a Jew and a rabbi—why He would speak to her, a Samaritan woman. Any other Jew would have gone thirsty (or gone another route). But Jesus wasn't any other Jew.

"If you knew the gift of God, and who it is who says to you, 'Give Me a drink,' you would have asked Him, and He would have given you living water," Jesus replied. In other words, the cultural barriers Jesus crossed were nothing compared to the spiritual barrier—God came to a sinner. If she realized this, it would be *her* doing the asking of Him! Jesus offered her "living water," Jeremiah's metaphor for a direct relationship with God.

Our group encircled the well, which stood about three feet high. We dipped from the bucket beside it and poured the dipper en masse into the abyss. We listened and counted, "One thousand one, one thousand two, one thous—" *Splash!* Over 70 feet deep. I thought of the woman's words.

"Sir, You have nothing to draw with and the well is deep; where then do You get that living water?" (John 4:11). Like Nicodemus, she thought only in the natural. So Jesus explained that "living water" means spiritual life.

"Everyone who drinks of this water will thirst again; but whoever drinks of the water that I will give him shall never thirst; but the water that I will give him will become in him a well of water springing up to eternal life" (John 4:13-14).

She still didn't connect the dots. So again, as He had done for Nicodemus, Jesus revealed her need.

"Go, call your husband, and come here."

"I have no husband."

"You have had five husbands, and the one whom you now have is not your husband; this you have said truly" (John 4:16-18).

Talk about revealing a need! Most women came to draw water in the mornings and evenings—the very reason she came here at noon. She tried to avoid her disgrace, to hide her sin, which everyone knew . . . but God still found her. He always does.

The world makes promises it can't keep. It says the reason we're unhappy is that we just haven't found the right *whatever* yet—the right spouse, the right hairdo, the right salary, the right entertainment system, the right church, the right pastor, the right Bible study, the right Bible, the right seminar, ad infinitum . . . ad nauseam.

You don't have to be without Christ to fall into the trap. Even those of us who do believe in Jesus can toss our buckets down the wrong wells. But God won't let us hide from reality; He loves us too much. He'll give us proddings, even piercings, to lead us to the truth we fear facing: God alone remains the source of satisfaction and the greatest motivation in our lives. Saint Augustine correctly observed, "Our heart does not rest until it rests in God."

When Jesus spoke to the woman about her deepest need, her mind stayed wedged in the realm of the natural. She sought purpose and security in relationships. Jesus' words to the woman—"Everyone who drinks of this water shall thirst again"—apply to more than water. They relate to everything—*everything*—we draw from in life for meaning and purpose apart from the One who spoke the words.

Cornered and uncomfortable, the Samaritan woman dodged the subject. Jesus graciously brought her back. Again, she sidestepped by saying that when the Messiah comes, *then* we'll know the truth. She figured that pulling the Messiah card was her ace in the hole. Jesus' final statement shook her to the core.

"I who speak to you am He" (John 4:26).

Okay, so . . . now what? No more excuses. Jesus had revealed her need for removal of her sin; He revealed the solution in living water. Would she believe Jesus' words?

Talk about timing. Just then, the disciples return with the burgers and fries, so the woman leaves the scene. Not only does she leave her water pot, but she also leaves the life she came with. She went to the people of the city she had previously avoided and told them about Jesus, the Messiah. Jesus stayed with the Samaritans two days before continuing on to Galilee. This would undoubtedly prepare the way for Peter, John and Philip to later return and preach again in Samaria (see Acts 8:4-25).

The woman had come to the well for water, and she left with living water. Oh, that we all would drop our water pots!

Before we departed Jacob's Well, I started to take a picture of it. The man behind the counter abruptly stopped me. "No pictures! This is a church!" He spoke as if I had spit on the floor, or worse.

I pointed to the racks of postcards beside him, most of which had pictures of the well. "And what about these?"

"You can buy these," he smiled.

A few minutes later, after most of our group headed for the bus, I got Cathy to ask the man if *she* could take a picture. He let her. *And in a church!*

After driving out of the valley, I pondered the Samaritans' confession: "We have heard for ourselves and know that this One is indeed the Savior of the world" (John 4:42). Jesus is the Savior of all . . . *even of Samaritans.*

—᠅—

Our bus climbed the hills rising out of the northern edge of the Jezreel Valley. A passenger pointed to a sign, written in Hebrew. "What does that say?"

I strained at the words: "Nazareth e-leet." We finished our ascent, crested and then descended into the bowl where sat the city of Jesus' day. We learned that "Nazareth Illit" simply means "Upper Nazareth"—as in elevation.

"Can any good thing come out of Nazareth?" (John 1:46). Nathanael's question crossed my mind as we drove.

We passed row after row of small unpainted homes in disrepair. They reminded me of my visits to Mexico as a boy and the country villages of Russia I saw as a missionary—very poor, very old and very crowded. We stayed at the elegant Nazareth Marriott, an awkward contrast to the poor dwellings we passed on our way in.

History has recorded precious little about the early centuries in Nazareth after Jesus lived there. One pilgrim of the sixth century inventively filled in the gaps by claiming that the Nazareth synagogue houses the book in which Jesus wrote His ABCs and a bench on which He sat (that only Christians can move). The Jewish women of Nazareth, he claimed, are better looking than any other Jewesses in the country!—supposedly Mary's gift to them.[1] But aside from the beautiful Church of the Annunciation, which commemorates Gabriel's announcement to Mary, Nazareth struggles to offer significant sites to see.

When Jesus came to Galilee from His journey up through Samaria, He began to preach the same message John the Baptist had preached before his imprisonment. Their message suggested an ending, or a *fulfillment*, of something old that God had promised long before Jesus: "The time is fulfilled, and the kingdom of God is at hand; repent and believe in the gospel" (Mark 1:15).

I try to imagine looking Jesus in the eyes as He preached. I want to think His stare would be penetrating, riveting, laser-like. As I looked at the local Jews during my time in Israel, I wondered, *Did Jesus look like him? Or maybe him?* Growing up, I had always imagined that Jesus had looked like the actor Robert Powell, a blue-eyed Caucasian with a cool British accent—speaking English. But if His initial encounters with people serve as any indication of reality, Jesus probably seemed a big disappointment. A rugged carpenter, sure. But He didn't look like a Messiah (see Isa. 53:2). He looked like the guy you grew up with.

When Jesus came to His hometown of Nazareth, He found a warm welcome—until His first sermon. He claimed to have fulfilled the messianic prophecy He had just read from Isaiah (see Luke 4:16-30). Then He claimed the Gentiles had more faith than they—the Jews—did! That didn't go over too well.

Enraged, His own people took Him to the edge of the Nazareth Ridge and wanted to hurl Him off into the Jezreel Valley. But He passed through their midst and left there. I bet that made for awkward subsequent holiday gatherings.

Just as Nazareth sits in a bowl with a ridge around it, so the shallow Sea of Galilee sits surrounded on all sides by towering hills. Today during times of drought, the 7-by-13-mile freshwater lake is at a lower level than in Jesus' time, making its exposed harbors easy to study.

During a drought in 1986, two brothers, sons of a fisherman, were walking along the shores of the Sea of Galilee where they grew up. One brother saw an old nail in the dirt, then another and another. Then they unearthed some ancient wood. They had discovered a boat from the time of Christ. Some sensationally dub it the "Jesus Boat."

We made our way to the Nof Ginosar museum, which houses the preserved first-century boat the brothers found. A small glass case displayed a scale model of the boat as we entered. "People were a lot smaller back then," someone clucked. Made of oak and cedars of Lebanon, built with mortise-and-tenon joinery, the 7-by-26-foot vessel could have held up to 15 men. Jesus and His disciples would have ridden in such a craft—a marvel to imagine.

I passed through the gift shop and bought the paperback novel *O Jerusalem!*—which I planned to devour after the ice cream I acquired. Outside, the group meandered to the boat docks. We boarded a bulky boat made entirely of wood with "Matthew" sloppily painted on the hull. The sailors pulled in the tires that cushioned the vessel from the dock, and we shoved off.

As we sailed on the Sea of Galilee, I stood at the bow and leaned over the edge, looking at the dark green water that parted against the keel below me. It looked like normal water . . . *Jesus walked on normal water*. The boat's cheap stereo system played loud, festive Jewish music. In the distance, several jet skis and wind sailors skimmed across the surface, and a white ski boat pulled a man on slalom. I would *love* to ski on the Sea of Galilee! That would be the closest I'd come to walking on water.

We slowed just off the north shore before a small gray church. Spring water flowed from a large pipe beside where the Jordan empties into the sea. The place has a Greek name, Heptapegon, meaning "place of seven springs"; but in Arabic it is called Tabgha ("tav-guh"). The springs attract fish to this part of the sea, and have for thousands of years. In fact, I saw a fisherman standing on the shore, holding his nets. At the sight of him, I tried to imagine the scene that took place here.

Simon Peter stood on the shore with his partners, James and John, cleaning their nets after a wasted night of fishing. Jesus selected Peter's boat as a makeshift pulpit and taught the people from the lake. Afterwards, Jesus turned to Peter.

"Put out into the deep water and let down your nets for a catch" (Luke 5:4). Reluctantly, Peter did so, possibly near where our boat was floating. The resulting catch produced enough fish to begin sinking two boats. Imagine two vessels, 7 by 26 feet each, sinking—that's a lot of fish!

More than any other Gospel writer, Luke portrayed Jesus as the "Son of Man," or God's ideal man. Only Luke recorded this first miraculous catch (see Luke 5:1-11), perhaps to reveal how Jesus was fulfilling God's original purpose for man: "Let Us make man in Our image, according to Our likeness; and let them rule over the fish of the sea" (Gen. 1:26).

Beside the shores of Tabgha, a dumbfounded Peter fell at Jesus' feet, fish still flopping all around them, and confessed: "Go away from me, Lord, for I am a sinful man" (Luke 5:8).

Jesus' response to Peter must have seemed as miraculous as the catch: "Do not fear, from now on you will be catching men" (v. 10).

Jesus accepted Peter despite his sin and gave him purpose and direction. Jesus had already met and called many of His disciples, including Peter, who apparently had returned to their livelihoods. But from this point, they would stay with Him until the end. They left everything and followed Jesus.

I could smell the fish before I saw them onshore. Dirty boats with tackle and cranes floated while moored to the docks at En Gev. One fisherman literally stood knee-deep in fish, shoveling spadefulls onto a vertical conveyor belt that hauled buckets of sardines, musht and barbels up to the ice. The place where we ate lunch served musht, often called "St. Peter's Fish." It's delightful to look at and loved by many people. But I prefer filets, so I ordered a slice of pizza.

—⁓—

Pink crepe myrtles spilled over the tall, iron gate. A blue sign in all caps announced our location: "CAPHARNAUM THE TOWN OF JESUS."

Jesus moved His base of operations from Nazareth to the bustling city of Capernaum, which straddled the "International Highway" beside the Sea of Galilee. The highway served as the first-century Internet or phone line. Whisper a word, and in a day, everyone within 20 miles could know it. (More about this major ancient trade route in chapter 4.)

I entered the gate, and the attendant immediately confiscated my video camera. "It looks professional," he explained, standing beside racks of postcards. "You can get it when you leave." I pouted the whole time. (On subsequent visits to Capernaum, I just took the lens shade off my camera. Then I was not "professional"! Now, however, the attendants require anyone who videos to pay $100.)

The ruins of the Capernaum synagogue date to a few centuries after the time of Christ. But they rest on top of the still-visible black basalt foundation of the first-century synagogue. Here Jesus drove out a demon and taught "as one having authority, and not as the scribes" (Mark 1:22). The interior bore a U-shaped seating arrangement with two rows of columns lining the center. Monks in brown frocks wandered in all directions and posed for pictures. I had my picture taken with one who apparently hadn't bathed in days.

A stone's throw outside the synagogue sits what looked like a spaceship hovering over the ruins of an ancient home. The structure covers the archaeological remains of Peter's house and affords, after entering, a bird's-eye view of the small dwelling. Here Jesus healed Peter's mother-in-law; here He cured those sick and possessed who pressed in by the door at sundown; here He departed long before daylight for a solitary place to pray (see Mark 1:29-35). Many sought Him for physical healing, but Jesus had a higher priority.

"Let us go somewhere else to the towns nearby, so that I may preach there also," Jesus told Peter and the others, "for that is what I came for" (Mark 1:38).

When Christ paced the northern shores of the Sea of Galilee, He had one theme on His lips: "the kingdom of God is at hand." His miracles served to *verify the message* and to give a foretaste of what He would do for those who enter His kingdom. Just as the worshippers who came to the wilderness Tabernacle had to be whole, so those who enter God's kingdom must be completely whole, spiritually and physically, for mere "flesh and blood cannot inherit the kingdom of God" (1 Cor. 15:50; see also 1 Cor. 15:51-53; cf. Lev. 15:31-33; 21:17-23).

In the same way Christ's resurrection would serve as a preview of every believer's resurrection, so every healing offered an example of what God will do on a cosmic scale for all believers—a foretaste of our glorification. We will be set free like a captive bird released over an open field (see Lev. 14:7). Before we enter Christ's holy presence, He "will transform our lowly bodies so that they will be like his glorious body" (Phil. 3:21, *NIV*).

The Jews knew all about the blessings of the Kingdom Jesus offered. But most ignored the requirement to enter it, which both John and Jesus preached: "Repent." Many folks didn't want to be born again. Once was enough. *I just need Jesus to fix my bad back and put bread on the table. Otherwise, I'm good.* Sounds a lot like many prayers today.

When a thick crowd around Peter's house kept some friends from bringing a paralytic to Jesus, they promptly dismantled the roof and lowered him into Jesus' presence. Before He healed the man, Jesus' words surprised everyone, "Son, your sins are forgiven" (Mark 2:5; see also Matt. 9:2; Luke 5:20). Jesus dealt with the man's greater need first, which drew critical, silent sneers from the scribes present.

"He is blaspheming; who can forgive sins but God alone?" (Mark 2:7). *And who else but God can read minds, guys?* Jesus revealed their thoughts and then used a miracle to confirm His words.

"But *so that you may know* that the Son of Man has authority on earth to forgive sins," Jesus turned to the paralytic, "I say to you, get up, pick up your pallet and go home" (Mark 2:10-11, emphasis added). The more difficult deed proved the lesser: When Jesus healed the man, it also meant Jesus could forgive sins. The miracle validated the message. And it proved that Jesus was God.

64

After calling Matthew to follow Him, Jesus celebrated at Matthew's house (see Matt. 9:9-13). The Pharisees, whose name probably means "separate ones," took issue with Jesus' disciples: "Why is your teacher eating with the tax collectors and 'sinners'?" (v. 11; see also Mark 2:16; Luke 5:30). In response, Jesus effectively told the Pharisees to go and read their Bibles: "But go and learn what this means: 'I desire compassion, and not sacrifice,' for I did not come to call the righteous, but sinners" (Matt. 9:13; cf. Hos. 6:6; 1 Tim. 1:15). Jesus again held up the stipulation of repentance required for entering God's kingdom (see Luke 5:32).

But the Pharisees had their own idea about what was required of people. In fact, the religious leaders observed oral traditions that added hundreds of rules to the Old Testament. Under Rabbi Judah in A.D. 200, these traditions eventually found their way to paper and became the Mishnah. For the Sabbath alone, tradition had 39 categories, with 6 subdivisions each, defining what qualified as "work." This one law had almost 240 applications. They had to work very hard to rest on the Sabbath!

During the second Passover of Jesus' ministry, He healed a man in Jerusalem on the Sabbath. This drew fire from the Pharisees, who felt that Jesus had disobeyed the command to rest on the Sabbath. Jesus told them again that they didn't know their Bibles (see Matt. 12:1-8; Mark 2:23-28; Luke 6:1-5; cf. Hos. 6:6). Jesus came to offer them the *real* meaning of the Sabbath—freedom from the futility of working to meet the Law's standard, and rest in Christ's finished work on the cross (see Matt. 11:29; Heb. 4:8-10). Ironically, the very Scriptures the leaders looked to for eternal life pointed to Jesus, but they refused to come to Him (see John 5:39,45-47).

Back in Galilee, in Capernaum's synagogue, the Pharisees and teachers of the Law watched to see if Jesus would heal on the Sabbath so that they might accuse Him. (But doesn't the fact that Jesus *could heal* prove something?) Jesus asked them whether it served the purpose of the Sabbath to do good or to do evil—to save life or to kill (see Mark 3:1-6). Their response?

You could hear crickets.

Deeply distressed over their stubborn hearts, Jesus healed the man. They were furious! Jesus' preaching and healing violated their long-standing traditions. If the popular Jesus kept this up, their whole system could collapse. In less than a year, the religious leaders went from questioning Jesus to accusing Him to plotting to get rid of Him. Miracle worker or not, He had to go. The honeymoon was over.

On the Sabbath, Jesus healed. And they plotted to kill. What's wrong with this picture?

We followed the sign to Route 90 and the Rosh Pinna Sill and approached a gentle, rolling hill between Tabgha and Capernaum, with fields of bananas and wildflowers sloping to the edge of the Sea of Galilee. Atop this "Mount of Beatitudes," the Franciscan Sisters constructed a church in 1939 (with the support of Italy's Mussolini!). Built of gray cinderblocks and white mortar, the simple chapel has an octagonal shape commemorating the eight beatitudes (see Matt. 5:3-10) and supports a stained dome topped with a cross.

Palm trees, colorful flowerbeds, Saint Augustine grass and plenty of shade make this a tranquil place to overlook the slope and the sea.

Shoreline of Tabgha beside the Sea of Galilee,
with Mount Arbel in the background.

The church atop the Mount of Beatitudes marks the traditional location for Jesus' Sermon on the Mount.

People quietly milled about as a college choir group sang the "Doxology" across the lawn. But the tranquility was brief.

As we stepped downstairs toward the garden theater, an annoying sound suddenly shot through my right ear. A nun appeared on the church's balcony, angry, loud and pointing at my camera. She had large glasses with a matching nose, a white starched-stiff habit that stretched from her forehead to the back of her shoulders, cuffs rolled up at the sleeves, and what looked like black house shoes. I had never had a nun yell at me before (perhaps this was Mussolini's daughter). Our tour organizer, Steve, went over and spoke with her.

In the spring of A.D. 31, after Passover, Jesus came up this mountain, sat down and began to teach those on the grass before Him. He covered a plethora of practical topics such as honesty, love, anger, adultery, revenge, giving, prayer and hypocrisy. But His message also taught what it took to enter the Kingdom He offered. And the standard was high.

"I say to you that unless your righteousness surpasses that of the scribes and Pharisees, you will not enter the kingdom of heaven. Therefore you are to be perfect, as your heavenly Father is perfect" (Matt. 5:20,48).

Jesus' statements reminded the people what the Tabernacle, the Temples and the prophets had taught them for centuries: "You shall be holy, for I the LORD your God am holy" (Lev. 19:2). The means of acquiring the holiness needed to enter the narrow gate that leads to life comes through knowing Jesus (see Matt. 7:13-14). Apart from Him, all good deeds—even miraculous ones—remain powerless to save.

Before we left the Mount of Beatitudes, Steve, a marvelous peacemaker, had the angry nun smiling.

"She's really a nice lady," he told us.

Perhaps he reminded her of the words of the sermon that made this place famous: "Blessed are the gentle, for they shall inherit the earth" (Matt. 5:5).

Everybody had expectations of Jesus, but He didn't dance to their tune.

In fact, He used just such a word picture to describe their reaction to Him (see Luke 7:32). Sure, Jesus preached well, and healings are always nice. But this carpenter from Nazareth *couldn't* be the Messiah. The crowds asked, "This man cannot be the Son of David, can he?" (Matt. 12:23). They expected a negative answer to their question. But then, how does He do miracles?

It was time for a public statement from the Pharisees. They had a ready answer.

"This man casts out demons only by Beelzebul the ruler of the demons" (Matt. 12:24). They attributed Jesus' miracles to the power of Satan rather than to the power of the Holy Spirit! Jesus told them that this view—of attributing Jesus' miracles to Satan—represents "an eternal sin" (see Matt. 12:31-32). What does that mean?

This "unpardonable sin" so often gets misapplied outside of its context: For some people, the thought is that refusing to believe in Jesus represents the *one* sin that God will not forgive. That's true, but *every* sin is unpardonable if a person refuses Jesus. The context of Jesus' statement was the miracles that validated His offer of the Kingdom (a critical observation). A rejection of the miracles' true source—the Holy Spirit—amounted to a rejection of Jesus' offer of the Kingdom.

The unpardonable sin, specifically, was a warning for that generation who saw Jesus' miracles and heard of His offer of the Kingdom. No one can commit this sin today. That generation of Israel had rejected Him and His offer of God's Kingdom on Earth, so He would reject them by postponing His offer. As He would later say, "Therefore I say to you, the Kingdom of God will be taken away from you, and be given to a nation producing the fruit of it" (Matt. 21:43). One day in the future, at Christ's Second Coming, Israel will believe . . . but for now, Jesus anticipated rejection.

"So prove it," the leaders essentially demanded. If Jesus' miracles came from God, the Pharisees wanted to see a miraculous sign.

I could italicize, underline and bold the following sentence and still fail to do justice to its importance: *The rulers' rejection of Jesus' offer of the Kingdom on that day represented the most determinative event in the ministry of Christ.* From this moment on, Jesus began to withdraw and postpone His offer. His answer to their demand for a sign confirmed this tragic pivot.

"An evil and adulterous generation craves for a sign; and yet no sign will be given to it but the sign of Jonah the prophet" (Matt. 12:39). In other words, they had already rejected His signs. He would show them no more miracles to validate His offer. None, that is, except one: the sign of Jonah, meaning Christ's resurrection after three days (see v. 40).

Like Israel of old, the leaders of Jesus' day still wanted a king like all the other nations. Jesus miserably failed their expectations.

Just then, Jesus' mother and brothers showed up outside. For support? Hardly. "They went out to take custody of Him; for they were saying, 'He has lost His senses'" (Mark 3:21). When Jesus heard they had come, His response revealed that He was closer in relationship to those who obeyed His message of repentance than to those whose blood He shared—a statement that extended beyond His family to the Jewish leaders of that "evil and adulterous generation" (see Matt. 12:46-50).

Our vehicle pulled to a stop before the early morning traffic could begin to blare. Near the base of the Mount of Beatitudes, our guide descended to the shoreline while the rest of us worked our way up the hill. I turned, sat down and listened. Birds, wind and silence. Our guide looked like a dot in the small cove along the shore, hundreds of yards below me. He began to read.

"Listen to this! Behold, the sower went out to sow; as he was sowing, some seed fell beside the road, and the birds came and ate it up" (Mark 4:3-4). He read the whole parable, and amazingly, I could hear every word. The site could have accommodated thousands of listening ears.

Scripture notes that on the *same day* the religious leaders attributed Jesus' miracles to Satan, Jesus went out to the lake, sat in a boat and "spoke many things to them in parables" (Matt. 13:3; see also vv. 1-2). The cove below me was the likely location of this event.

The distance between the Mount of Beatitudes and the small cove below it amounted to a few hundred yards. But the distance between the reasons for the messages Jesus preached in these two places has stretched over 2,000 years. In the Sermon on the Mount, Jesus shot straight with the people about the kingdom of God and how to get in. But after the leaders' public rejection of Him, Jesus' parables introduced a radical departure from how He had been teaching.

The disciples recognized this change and questioned Him about it. He answered that parables revealed truth to those who were seeking it but concealed truth from those who weren't (see Matt. 13:10-17). The parables allowed Jesus still to teach publicly without heaping greater condemnation on those who refused to believe. How gracious!

"He who has ears, let him hear," Jesus concluded (Matt. 13:9). God had always told Israel, beginning with their priests, that a life devoted to God has ears to hear, hands to work and feet to follow Him (see Lev. 8:22-24; Ps. 78:1-2).

In light of Israel's leaders' rejection of the offer of the Kingdom, Jesus' whole tactic in ministry changed. From then on, He mostly preached in parables. Also, Jesus' miracles became less public affirmations of His message and more private acts of mercy and instruction for His disciples (see Luke 8:22-25,51-56).

It would have made a great scene in a James Dean movie: The black-sheep son is run out of town after his audacious public speech offends his town. But he later boldly strolls back into the city, straight to the town hall, and speaks again.

When Jesus came again to His hometown of Nazareth, He certainly heard some snickers on His way to the synagogue. But when He began teaching, the snickers turned to scoffing.

"'Where did this man get these things, and what is this wisdom given to Him, and such miracles as these performed by His hands? Is not this the carpenter, the son of Mary, and brother of James and Joses and Judas and Simon? Are not His sisters here with us?' And they took offense at Him" (Mark 6:2-3).

Familiarity breeds contempt, yes. And blind arrogance.

Rather than being driven to discover the meaning behind the miracles and wisdom, the Nazarenes took offense that the little local-yokel Jesus would dare to be remarkable. *You can't be that special—I know your family.* It's always easier to snub the truth than to repent. Proverbs offers wisdom to every convert who dares to grow and let it show: "When a wise man has a controversy with a foolish man, the foolish man either rages or laughs, and there is no rest" (Prov. 29:9). In other words, foolish people will either get angry or blow you off, but you'll never convince them.

"Can any good thing come out of Nazareth?" Apparently, even those from Nazareth answered "No!"

The only time the Gospels speak of Jesus' marveling comes in reference to the stubborn unbelief of His hometown (see Mark 6:6). Their lack of faith, not His lack of power, kept Jesus from doing many miracles in Nazareth. He simply refused to perform.

Jesus had sent out the 12 disciples He had appointed as "apostles" (meaning "sent ones") to extend His ministry throughout Galilee by teaching, preaching and healing (Mark 3:13-19; Luke 6:12-16). Word of Christ's ministry even reached as far south as the Dead Sea and east to Machaerus, where John the Baptist sat staring at his prison walls, wondering.

Put yourself in John's cell for a moment. He had preached about the Messiah's kingdom coming with power and justice. But instead, John found himself unfairly wasting away in prison for a year. John had taught that Christ would cut down and burn "every tree that does not bear good fruit" and "thoroughly clear His threshing floor" (see Matt. 3:10-12). Instead, Jesus' ministry centered on preaching and acts of mercy. Gentle Jesus hardly seemed the political Deliverer everyone expected.

At least John took his struggle with Jesus to its source. Many others just flat out rejected Him, in spite of the obvious miracles (see Matt. 11:20-24). Unable to reconcile the contradictions, imprisoned in his thoughts, John doubted his own sermon. And by doubting Jesus,

John also doubted himself and the whole purpose for his life. In desperation, John sent messengers to Jesus to ask, "Are You the Expected One, or shall we look for someone else?" (Matt. 11:3; see also Luke 7:19-20).

In other words, the Expected One had certain expectations on Him. Jesus had failed to meet them.

I've always been amazed that even though the Scriptures had predicted Jesus' life and ministry for centuries, He seemed to disappoint everyone He met. His parents misunderstood Him; His leaders thought Him possessed; His family called Him crazy; and His hometown found Him offensive. Even His prophetic forerunner had second thoughts!

John's question to Jesus finds its roots in the heart of every believer who struggles with how God should act. Have you ever felt as if God let you down? Have you ever felt as if life doesn't really jibe with Scripture—that the "good news" doesn't really "work" in the real world?

In those moments of struggle, or perhaps right now, ask yourself, *If the gospel "worked," what would it look like? What do I expect from it?*

The Lord uses trials to change us—sure, we know this (see Rom. 5:3-4). But we also expect that after we do change, God will remove the circumstances that caused the change. After all, the trials have served their purpose, right? We expect that if we truly surrender, our submission will unlock the dam for God's blessings to flow. We expect that the reward of repentance is relief, or at least some respite from struggle.

But God views our repentance itself as the prize. *Our changed life is the reward* this side of heaven. That perspective often takes decades to learn (see James 1:2-4). God often chooses to glorify Himself by spotlighting the integrity of a believer in a situation where knots remain untied. A watching world wonders at such a life.

When we come face to face with our false expectations of Jesus, a crisis often occurs—or may I suggest that a crisis is *required*—before God can remove the dross of our false hopes and help us see Him for who He really is.

Even when our expectations are biblical, as John's were, we still see them through the lens of impatience. We expect that if God has promised to act, He should act *now!* As if God's whole universe exists for us—or as if we know best *when* we need what we need.

Jesus spoke clearly, but most still misunderstood Him. He balanced perfect priorities, but others still demanded their agendas. He treated people with equity, but He received mistreatment. He offered life, but He received death. See the pattern? Experiencing disappointment with a perfect God should suggest where the true problem lies.

We should always hesitate to assume the Gospel doesn't work when we simply cannot see the big picture. A contradiction in God's Word means a contradiction in God—or so it might seem. But the Lord reminded Judah, "For as the heavens are higher than the earth, so are My ways higher than your ways and My thoughts than your thoughts" (Isa. 55:9). When we struggle to connect truth with life, we must embrace the limitations of our understanding . . . and the limitlessness of God's. Our inability to understand Jesus should give cause for worship, not cause for doubt.

Jesus graciously challenged John the Baptist to shape his expectations from the Word of God and not from the circumstances that seemed to contradict it: "Blessed is he who does not take offense at Me" (Matt. 11:6). John's lesson leaves a lingering application for us: We should never allow our expectations of Jesus to weaken our confidence in Him—even when we don't fully understand how He will work it all out. Because this life is not the end of the story.

Jesus received news of John's execution at about the time the disciples returned from their mission. Jesus knew what John's death implied. They had shared the same message; they would share the same fate. The death of John foreshadowed the death of Jesus.

Ironically, while the leaders failed to see that Jesus had offered the Kingdom, the disciples failed to see that Jesus was postponing the Kingdom. To them, all seemed full-steam ahead. The disciples had their own expectations of Jesus, and they would not give them up easily.

Jesus would now spend the bulk of His time preparing the disciples for something new—something they never expected to happen.

Note

1. John Wilkinson, *Egeria's Travels to the Holy Land,* rev. ed. (Warnimster, England: Aris and Phillips; Jerusalem, Israel: Ariel, 1981), p. 5.

CHAPTER FOUR

PREPARING THE DIRTY DOZEN

Many of His disciples withdrew and were not walking with Him anymore.
So Jesus said to the twelve, "You do not want to go away also, do you?"
Simon Peter answered Him, "Lord, to whom shall we go?
You have words of eternal life."

JOHN 6:66-68

"DANGER MINES!" Some signs you don't have to read twice.

This one hung on a fence beside the ruins of et-Tell, ancient Bethsaida, as a mute reminder of the conflicts the Golan Heights have seen. I guess it's easier to hang up a sign than to dig up the mines.

The path led us along the ruins of Bethsaida's basalt houses, which lay clumped together like honeycomb. To my right, trees with peeling bark suspended makeshift sieves, which appeared little more than wooden frames with screens attached. Several archaeologists hovered over these sifters and separated dirt from debris.

I remembered an archaeological dig in which Cathy and I participated down by Tel Maresha. We squatted with our picks in an Idumean cave carved out in the first century. I could see the original tool markings still on the cave walls. Cathy found a jar handle, fully intact. I unearthed some pottery shards with fingerprints on them. I held them close and compared the pottery's prints to my own. Somehow the shards bridged a 2,000-year-old emotional gap between me and the potter; he or she seemed more real to me with fingerprints.

"Where are you from?" we asked one of the volunteer archaeologists who stood over a sifter. A young man, he had blonde hair, no shirt and leather gloves.

"Alaska." When he saw that we took his picture, he added, "Hey, can I have a copy of that?"

Peter, Andrew and Philip grew up in Bethsaida (see John 1:44). The city's name means "house of fish," and its location, quite distant from the Sea of Galilee, would have required of these three fishermen a daily commute. The city sat east of the Jordan River, in Herod Philip's territory, and the fishermen would have been charged extra taxes to bring their catches home across the border. So to avoid these headaches, they eventually relocated their families to Capernaum.

We followed the footpath to an open shelter covered with dead, dried palm fronds and sat in its shade on benches. As we opened our Bibles to read, smoke from some distant fire filled my nostrils. I scanned beyond the basalt rocks and groves of trees to the vast, desolate plain southeast of Bethsaida.

A massive crowd gathered near here to be with Jesus (see Luke 9:10-11). He felt compassion for them "because they were like sheep without a shepherd; and He began to teach them many things" (Mark 6:34). But as suppertime approached and stomachs began to rumble, the disciples sensed a growing uneasiness about the crowds. They offered Jesus a suggestion.

"Send them away," they told Jesus, "so that they may go into the surrounding countryside and villages and buy themselves something to eat" (Mark 6:36).

One of those nearby villages was Gamla, which means "camel," because its topography resembled a hump. The village also had plenty of drinking water from natural springs that flowed from the Golan Heights. When I visited Gamla, a lone vulture circled me. *What does he want?* I wondered. Probably the same thing the people needed that day from Jesus—food.

The disciples' suggestion seemed perfectly reasonable, even caring and responsible. The people need to eat, so send them away to forage. Jesus' reply shot panic into their minds.

"*You* give them something to eat" (Matt. 14:16; Mark 6:37; Luke 9:13, emphasis added).

Twelve jaws dropped in perfect synchronization. Philip voiced what they all were thinking: "Eight months' wages would buy everybody little more than a bite!" Andrew found a boy with a sack lunch—five loaves and two fish—but added the obvious, "But what are these for so many people?" (John 6:7-9).

The disciples focused on the inadequacy of *their* resources. But if Christ called the disciples to feed thousands with their inadequate supply, Jesus must have meant to show that the disciples had a source they had overlooked.

The Lord had His men seat the crowds on the green grass. After giving thanks, Jesus kept giving the food to the disciples to set before the people. After everyone ate, Jesus' men each picked up a basket of leftovers.

Byzantine believers mistook the miracle as happening near Tabgha and commemorated the event with a beautiful mosaic in the modern Church of the Multiplication of the Loaves and Fishes (there's a great name for your next church plant). We call this miracle the "feeding of the 5,000." But that number represented just the men; women and children also ate (see Matt. 14:21). A conservative estimate puts the entire crowd at well over 10,000. Why mention numbers? Ironically, to show that they don't matter. They don't limit God—a principle repeatedly proven in the Old Testament (see Num. 11:22-23; 1 Sam. 14:6; 2 Kings 4:42-44).

But the numbers also reveal something else. If the disciples distributed food to at least 10,000 people, then each disciple would have had to carry food for 833 folks. Obviously, this took more than one trip. In other words, Jesus was teaching His men that ministry required them to come *continually* to Jesus with their overwhelming needs, and He would meet them in abundance (an obvious lesson, but one that is very hard to learn!).

This miracle represents the *only miracle* that appears in all four Gospels—other than the resurrection. Why so significant? Without the disciples realizing it, Jesus had begun to train His 12 men how to do ministry in the age of the Church. The lessons the disciples learned by handing out food revealed how to feed the Word of God to Jesus' sheep.

The word "disciple" comes from the Greek term *mathetes*, from which we get our word "mathematics." It simply means "student." But Jesus didn't call these men to follow Him to a classroom. Jesus' three-and-a-half year curriculum contained more than lectures. The program had labs as well. In fact, after this miracle, Jesus "immediately" put the disciples in a boat and pointed them northwest across the lake—without Him (see Matt. 14:22; Mark 6:45).

Time for a pop-quiz.

The Sea of Galilee was—and still is—notorious for unexpected storms. A squall in March 1992 sent 10-foot-high waves crashing into downtown Tiberias, causing significant damage. Imagine the panic of the disciples riding swells that high in a small boat!

Jesus remained alone on land and prayed. Then, sometime between 3 and 6 A.M., He came to the disciples by "walking on the sea" (Matt. 14:25; Mark 6:48; John 6:19). But instead of expecting their miracle-working Lord, the dozen on board assumed Jesus was, of all things, a ghost! He comforted them in reply, got in the boat and stilled the storm. Then Mark wrote what has always seemed an unusual line to me: "They were utterly astonished, for they had not gained any insight from the incident of the loaves, but their heart was hardened" (Mark 6:51-52).

Academic tests determine how much information we know. But God's tests reveal how much information we apply. Jesus intended that the lesson of the loaves be applied to the lab on the lake. In both instances, the disciples' own efforts to do what Jesus had commanded proved futile: They had to learn to depend on Him for the impossible tasks (see Mark 10:27).

Often in the Gospels, the disciples seem as dumb as stumps. But does knowing more than they do make us more faithful? Remember, lectures and labs go together. Knowledge serves no purpose without the will and the heart to obey.

If we're honest, I think we'll see that we resemble these men. The unrealistic expectations they had, which Jesus revealed, we also store in abundance. We have *our* agenda for how best to "serve God." All other events—especially storms—just get in the way.

"Their heart was hardened," Mark wrote—as if the disciples had one heart. These men didn't expect Jesus to teach them about their inadequacy and dependency. Jesus had chosen the Twelve from out of all the multitudes who followed Him. They felt special. And as such, they expected special treatment. The storm struck them as strange because they expected Christ to give them privileged places in His kingdom. They did not anticipate Christ assigning struggles to change their hard heart. *What for? Hasn't He already chosen us? What else is there to do but rule?*

After the Jerusalem Passover in mid-April of A.D. 32, Jesus would spend His final year reshaping the expectations of these men.

—⁊⁊⁊—

Israel burst with life as we traveled through the Dothan Pass that May.

Grapes grew in volleyball-sized clusters atop walls where foxes couldn't reach. Firm purple plums as big as golf balls had a white haze over their surface. Furrows ran horizontal on the slopes beside terraced groves, with olives as large and green as the grapes. Gleaners erected makeshift shelters to rest in, reminding me of Ruth gleaning in Boaz's field (see Ruth 2:7). Machines winnowed wheat and had it cut, bundled and tied. Fig trees looked just like the one in our backyard (plants really do reproduce after their kind). As we journeyed through these lush fields near Dothan, I thought of Joseph, who had been sold by his brothers there to the Ishmaelite traders as they traveled the International Highway south to Egypt (see Gen. 37:25-28).

We exited the Dothan Pass and the Mount Carmel Range into the broad expanse of the Jezreel Valley. We passed cultivated fields and clumps of houses that alternated like the colors of a checkerboard. I saw workers busy among squash plants, tomatoes, corn, sunflowers and hay prepared for sheaves—all in rows of parallel lines. No wonder they call this area the "breadbasket of Israel." Even in biblical times, with its fertile fields and easy access to the International Highway, northern Israel enjoyed steady commerce and prosperity with the nations—a strength that became a spiritual weakness.

After Passover, Jesus led His disciples north through this same fertile valley, about this same time of year, in late spring. I wonder if the words of Isaiah 28 echoed off the valley walls as they ricocheted off of the hard hearts of the leaders of Isaiah's day: "The proud crown of the drunkards of Ephraim is trodden under foot. And the fading

79

flower of its glorious beauty, which is at the head of the fertile valley, will be like the first-ripe fig prior to summer, which one sees, and as soon as it is in his hand, he swallows it" (Isa. 28:3-4).

God compared the Jewish leaders of the doomed Northern Kingdom to those who abused its fertility by getting drunk off its grapes. They interpreted Isaiah's words as unintelligible gibberish, childish nonsense (see Isa. 28:9-12). Later, the apostle Paul quoted this passage to show that unintelligible foreign languages (called "tongues") acted as a sign of the unwillingness of the Jews to believe God's message (see 1 Cor. 14:21; see also Acts 2:13 where, ironically, the first occurrence of tongues came with the accusation of drunkenness). Peter later quoted Isaiah 28 as well, referring to Jesus as "a precious corner stone, and he who believes in Him will not be disappointed" (1 Pet. 2:6; cf. Isa. 28:16).

But Peter had a long way to go before he had such insight.

Jesus began to expand His disciples' understanding of their future mission by entering Gentile territories, namely Tyre and Sidon by the Mediterranean Sea, and the Decapolis southeast of the Sea of Galilee (see Matt. 15:21-38; Mark 7:24–8:9). In this latter region, Jesus healed a deaf and dumb man privately, using spit. Then He multiplied the fish and loaves again—but this time for 4,000 Gentiles.

Later, in a boat on the Sea of Galilee, the disciples realized that they had forgotten to bring bread. Jesus used their lack of bread to teach a spiritual lesson: "Do you *not yet see* or understand? Do you have a hardened heart? Having eyes, *do you not see*? And having ears, *do you not hear*? Do you not yet understand?" (Mark 8:17-18,21, emphases added). Notice my emphases in His questions. Jesus compared seeing and hearing to understanding. He likened sight to insight, and then told them they lacked it. They had a hardened heart, the same one they had exhibited on the boat ride after the feeding of the 5,000. So Jesus took them back to where that miracle had occurred.

Some signs you don't have to read twice. Others you can stare at all day and still miss. The "DANGER MINES!" sign on the fence at Bethsaida made me think of another sign displayed there. Jesus gave the sign to the disciples, but they closed their eyes and walked blindly into the minefield of their own expectations.

As they came to Bethsaida, the hometown of Peter, Andrew and Philip, they brought a blind man to Jesus for healing. Maybe they grew up with him. Jesus led the blind man out of the city and then spit in his eyes. Can you imagine? After touching him, Jesus asked him a question that He also intended the disciples to consider.

"Do you see anything?" (Mark 8:23). The blind man replied that he did, but everything looked blurry. So Jesus touched him again, and he saw perfectly. Why the two-stage miracle? Was it an "off day" for Jesus? Remember, miracles confirmed a message—and Jesus was preaching to His men. But they misread the sign.

The dirty dozen had just experienced Jesus giving healing to two men: one who couldn't hear and one who couldn't see. Both miracles Jesus performed privately and with spit. Between these miracles came the stinging rebuke in the boat: "Having eyes, do you not see? And having ears, do you not hear?" Talk about missing a sign!

The bottom line? The disciples understood who Jesus was, but only partially. They saw Him through the blur of their own expectations. So the Lord took them north in order to clear the fog. Perhaps He should have spit in their eyes for good measure.

We headed north along the same ground Jesus took, real estate that made Israel the political desire of every superpower in antiquity. Driving the ancient International Highway felt like driving through the Bible. I looked over at one jet-lagged passenger who was fast asleep. *How can he sleep?!* I wanted to shake him and shout: " 'Awake, sleeper, and Christ will shine on you!' Look, don't you realize where you are? The International Highway!" But regrettably, I let him slumber.

This vast artery of transport was the major north-south trade route that stretched from the Fertile Crescent all the way to Egypt, running the entire length of Israel. Israel stood at the crossroads of three continents—Asia, Africa and Europe—and the oceans forced all who traveled to and from these continents by land to traverse Israel.

Thus, the armies of Egypt, Assyria, Babylon, Media-Persia, Greece and Rome all invaded Israel in order to control the International Highway—the *Via Maris*, or "Way of the Sea."

Even today, Israel serves as the passageway for large, high-flying birds that prefer not to migrate over the seas. Literally hundreds of thousands of steppe and spotted eagles, black and white storks, steppe and honey buzzards, black kites and Levant sparrowhawks soar over the Holy Land in their biannual migrations to and from East Africa.

Geographical chokepoints along the ancient international route forced all traffic to pass well-fortified cities. These stood to control all travel, trade and tariffs. In Israel's glory days, Solomon fortified Hazor, Megiddo and Gezer—cities critical to national security along the highway (see 1 Kings 9:15). I have seen the city gates that Solomon built in these three cities—all tripartite gates and nearly identical.

The deadbolt for northern Israel in the Old Testament was Hazor. Two hundred acres huge in its heyday, Hazor stood by the Via Maris as a critical line of defense. During the conquest of Canaan, Hazor was the only city Joshua burned other than Jericho. Two hundred years later, Deborah and Barak did the same. During the time of the divided kingdoms, Ben-hadad of Aram invaded Israel via Hazor, and the Assyrian King Tiglath-pileser III eventually carried Israel off to exile, leaving Hazor in ruins.

Atop this most massive tell in Israel (a "tell" is a mound formed over hundreds of years by the repeated destruction of a city and its continual rebuilding on top of the accumulated ruins), I stood among beautiful yellow blooms that gave evidence of life where so many people had died. I looked to the east, where the modern highway ran along the same ground the international artery did in antiquity. When Jesus passed Hazor on His way north, the ancient city stood as but a meager police fort. But its presence would have reminded the disciples of the foreign invasions Israel had suffered. It probably stirred patriotic passions against the current occupying power in Israel—Rome. And the reminder of Jesus' offer to Israel likely put a spring in their step: "The kingdom of God is at hand" (Mark 1:15).

We continued north along the ancient path and stopped briefly before the Lebanese border at Metulla. I got out to stretch my legs and looked back, dead south. Sheba's rebellion against King David came to an end at the mound before me, with a wise woman hurling Sheba's head to Joab over the wall of Abel Beth-maacah (see 2 Sam. 20:14-22).

"Long ago they used to say, 'Get your answer at Abel,'" the woman told Joab (2 Sam. 20:18, *NIV*). But the answer Jesus sought would come a few miles east of there. He had a question indeed for His disciples—the whole purpose for their journey north. And we were almost there.

We turned east at Abel Beth-maacah into the idolatrous city of Dan, or Tel Dan. Walking around the tell felt like traipsing through the American northwest. Cool, green and shady, it looked like none of the rest of Israel. The uneven, rocky pathways and shaded trails encircled the ancient tell and crisscrossed the Dan Spring. The spring flows from the base of Mount Hermon and remains the longest and most important source of the Jordan River. I paused to grin before a wooden sign painted in Hebrew: "Garden of Eden." It must have seemed that way to the tribe of Dan.

After abandoning their God-given inheritance down south, the tribe of Dan migrated to this fertile area, also abandoning their worship of God. While the Tabernacle remained at Shiloh, the Danites knelt before a graven image in their new digs up north—with the grandson of Moses, of all people, serving as priest (see Judg. 18:30).

Centuries later, King Jeroboam repeated the folly. While Solomon's Temple stood in Jerusalem, Jeroboam sanctioned the worship of two golden calves, one in Dan at a high place, which archaeologists have discovered (see 1 Kings 12:26-30). Jeroboam acted out of fear that "the kingdom will return to the house of David" (v. 26). Ironically—and I love this—the single secular source of proof for the historical existence of David came from an archaeological discovery in Tel Dan! In the Israel Museum, I have seen the Dan Stele, a large stone clearly inscribed with the words "the house of David." I love God's sense of humor.

83

In Israel, where there's water, there's life. I've also noticed that where there's water, there are teenagers! Wherever a natural spring forms a pool, teenagers cavort—from the many fords at Tel Dan all the way down south to En Gedi, where the ibex still roam the hills with their piercing brown eyes and sturdy feet. I probably would have jumped in the water too if I didn't have to get back on the bus. It looked refreshing.

Our motor coach pulled off Route 99 and rolled to a stop at Banias, or Caesarea Philippi, at the foot of Mount Hermon. We walked a shaded path where rock badgers, or hyraxes, scampered back into their crags. Hebrew poetry considered these creatures wise because they make their sanctuary in a safe place (see Ps. 104:18; Prov. 30:26). But the Law also labeled them unclean (Lev. 11:5; Deut. 14:7), a designation more befitting the idolatrous site where I saw them.

I stood before the mouth of a large cave from which a cold, crystal-clear stream flowed westward, then southward, helping to form the headwaters of the Jordan River. Niches carved to the right of the cave used to hold statues of idols dedicated to the Greek god Pan—the half man, half goat who played the panpipe. The site's present name, Banias, comes from *Paneas* (for Pan). In the time of Jesus, Herod Philip named the city Caesarea Philippi after himself and Caesar.

Jesus brought the Twelve all the way up to the pagan region of Caesarea Philippi and tossed them His question.

"Who do people say that the Son of Man is?" (Matt. 16:13).

The question Jesus asked His disciples came in the geographical context of idolatry and spiritual compromise—a history the disciples would have known well. Their answer reflected the popular opinion that Jesus was a man—a good man, a moral teacher, whom some would even call a prophet (see Matt. 16:14). This view still exists to-day among those who favor idols.

Then Jesus pitched them a fastball: "But who do *you* say that I am?" (Matt. 16:15).

Simon Peter stepped up to the plate and swung for the fence: "You are the Christ, the Son of the living God" (Matt. 16:16).

Jesus commended Peter for his insight. Then the Lord uttered a word He had never used before: "I will build My *church*; and the gates of Hades will not overpower it" (Matt. 16:18, emphasis added). For over two-and-a-half years Jesus had been preaching the kingdom of God, which had been promised for centuries. But now Jesus began teaching His men about a new, temporary form of God's kingdom, one that included a "mystery" in the Old Testament—the Church (Mark 4:11; Rom. 11:25; 16:25; Eph. 3:9; Col. 1:26-27).

The disciples had a correct view of *who* Jesus was—the Messiah, or Christ, God's Son—but they still saw Jesus' *mission* in a fog. They had no idea that Jesus would put Israel's kingdom program on hold and, in the meantime, build His Church. They only saw the Messiah in terms of His Kingship . . . and themselves as vice-regents. They knew only half the truth about Jesus—the half they wanted to know.

"From that time," Matthew wrote, "Jesus began to show His disciples that He must go to Jerusalem, and suffer many things from the elders and chief priests and scribes, and be killed, and be raised up on the third day" (Matt. 16:21). That day marked a pivot that would forever change these men.

85

Try to imagine the Twelve hearing for the first time what seems like old news to us. Jesus had never spoken to them so plainly before about His death and resurrection. Jesus introduced the Church, a brand-new mission. To boot, Jesus commanded them to tell no one He was the Christ (see Matt. 16:20). All of this must have seemed exceedingly strange—especially the part about Jesus dying.

Peter could stand it no longer. On the heels of his great confession, he opened his mouth again and put both heels in it: "God forbid it, Lord! This shall never happen to You" (Matt. 16:22). Peter rebuked Jesus!

The last time Jesus heard words like that, He stood on a high mountain where Satan offered Him the fast track to glory without the cross. But this time Satan spoke through the lips of Jesus' trusted friend. The Savior still recognized the source of the temptation, however, and addressed Peter in response to Satan.

"Get behind Me, Satan! You are a stumbling block to Me; for you are not setting your mind on God's interests, but man's. . . . If anyone

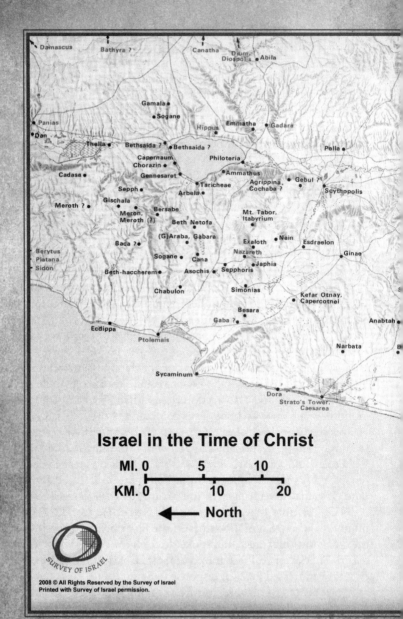

Israel in the Time of Christ

MI. 0   5   10

KM. 0   10   20

← North

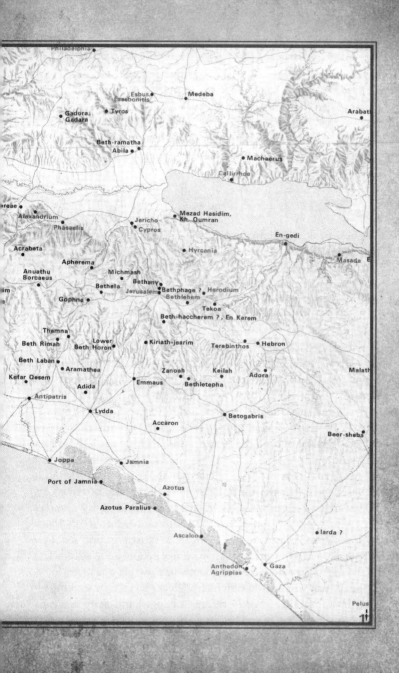

wishes to come after Me, he must deny himself, and take up his cross and follow Me" (Matt. 16:23-24; see also Mark 8:33).

Jesus added that the disciples' roles were also to be very different from what they had expected. Before they would follow Him to the throne, they would follow Him to the cross. Just as He would take up His cross, so they would take up theirs. And they impulsively recoiled.

What a terribly confusing moment.

—∿—

The highest peak inside modern Israel's borders is Mount Hermon, which rises 9,230 feet above sea level. The only experience more exhilarating than waterskiing on the Sea of Galilee would be snow skiing on Mount Hermon—a sport actually done in the winter! Imagine the oddity of the statement "We're going snow skiing in Israel this year." Picture also an ultra-orthodox Jew wearing his black garb and red ski boots! I've seen pictures.

We ascended the snow-capped mountain slowly and stopped partway up near the medieval castle called Nimrod's Fortress. On this cool, clear day, I could see for miles. Looking up, the mountain seemed to summit in heaven. Looking back down the long, slow grade, I could make out the areas of Dan and Caesarea Philippi below me. From there, Jesus brought three of His confused disciples up on the slopes of a "high mountain," probably Mount Hermon on which I stood.

Six days after He dropped the bomb about His death in Jerusalem, Jesus gave affirmation to Peter, James and John of His glory, divine nature and coming Kingdom (see Matt. 16:28–17:8). The text says Jesus was "transfigured" on the mountain (Matt. 17:2; Mark 9:2). We're so used to calling this event "the transfiguration" that we don't realize we're using an English word few people understand. The original Greek reads *metamorphao*, from which we get our word "metamorphosis," one definition of which Webster gives as "a striking alteration in appearance."[1] *Meta* means "change" and *morphe* means "form." Jesus' face became as bright as the sun and His garments as white as lightning. Try to picture that without squinting.

Jesus revealed His true glory, which His flesh had concealed like the veil of the Tabernacle had hidden God's glory (see Heb. 10:20). Both John and Peter never forgot this moment and would write of it in their epistles: "We have seen His glory" (John 1:14). "We were eye-witnesses of His majesty. . . . We were with Him on the holy mountain" (2 Pet. 1:16-18).

Suddenly, Moses and Elijah also appeared in glorious cameo appearances. They spoke of Jesus' "departure" at Jerusalem, the very event Jesus had just revealed to His disciples in Caesarea Philippi (see Luke 9:31). Remember Peter's earlier response? When Jesus spoke of the cross, Peter blurted in favor of the Kingdom. He did it again here: "Lord, it is good for us to be here; if You wish, I will make three tabernacles here, one for You, and one for Moses, and one for Elijah" (Matt. 17:4).

What was Peter suggesting? The prophet Zechariah had written that when the Messiah reigns on the earth, He will require all nations to come and celebrate the Feast of Booths, or Feast of the Tabernacles (see Zech. 14:16-19). Peter was pushing again for the Kingdom!

But even before Peter could finish his words, God the Father interrupted: "This is My beloved Son, with whom I am well-pleased; listen to Him!" (Matt. 17:5). The disciples fell facedown in a coil of terror. I guess so!

How utterly different this scene was from the last time the Father uttered that statement. Just before Jesus' temptation, the Father commended Jesus' holy life at His baptism in the Jordan River. Now, as Jesus anticipated His crucifixion, the Father commended Jesus again at His transfiguration.

These two scenes offer a striking contrast. One, the highest elevation of Jesus' ministry; the other, the lowest on Earth. One took place in the north; the other occurred in the south. One area was cool, lush and attractive; the other was hot, desolate and uninviting. One represented the beginning of the Jordan River; the other was the end of it. One location had Moses and Elijah appearing in glory; the other saw Moses and Elijah depart this earth to go to glory!

But these two scenes also had unifying elements. In addition to the Father's commendations, these events transpired adjacent to Satan's efforts to get Jesus to skirt the cross and head straight for glory. In fact, apart from the transfiguration, the only other time Matthew's Gospel mentions a "high mountain" occurs at the temptation when Satan took Jesus "to a very high mountain and showed Him all the kingdoms of the world and their glory" (Matt. 4:8).

We often find ourselves wandering in the valley between these two mountains, don't we? Between temptation and transfiguration—a place near Satan and a place near God. Between a place filled with hopeless desperation, weakness and frustration, where God seems so distant and His goodness a farce—and a place where God's presence seems so palpable, so reassuring, so good, so satisfying that we're convinced He is all we'll ever need. Oh, those magnificent moments!

Today's hardships can distract us from tomorrow's hope. We can get so obsessed with the weight of our cross that we forget Jesus showed us what lies beyond it. Jesus took His disciples to the mount of transfiguration to show them the glory on the other side of the struggle. This would prove critical for them in the days and years ahead—a lesson in motivation and hope Peter would return to again and again in his writings (see 1 Pet. 1:3-9,13; 4:13; 5:1; 2 Pet. 1:16-19). The transfiguration gives us hope because it shows us our future. And it's a good one.

Hope helped Jesus Himself endure His cross as well. How? He endured it "for the joy set before Him" (Heb. 12:2). Just like Christ, we *always* have to have a joy set before us. Daily. Constantly. Otherwise we will live bitter, discontented and frustrated lives (see Matt. 5:12; Rom. 12:12; 1 Pet. 1:3-9). The transfiguration promises a glorious future and therefore frees us to focus on God's interests rather than man's.

But there's more. As much as we'd like to build a few tabernacles on the mount of Christ's glorious presence and camp with Jesus until the Rapture, remember that He took His disciples back down the mountain into the struggles of the valley (see Matt. 17:9-21). Remember also that the Spirit led Jesus into the wilderness of temptation after His baptism.

The Kingdom *will* come indeed—Jesus showed the disciples that—but first they had a cross to bear. So do we. "If anyone wishes to come after Me, let him deny himself, and take up his cross and follow Me" (Mark 8:34).

The transfiguration confirmed that the only way *to* glory comes *through* the cross. There's no going around it. Even in the presence of Christ's glory on the mountain, Moses and Elijah spoke of Christ's death, or "departure"—literally, in the Greek, His *exodus* (Luke 9:31)—a nice literary touch with Moses standing there.

Following Jesus requires a denial of the will. Peter's passion had been to pursue *his* interests, not God's. Essentially he prayed, "My kingdom come, my will be done!" Biblical self-denial means more than denying yourself *something*, such as pecan pie; it means denying your *self*. It requires a mindset of putting God's desires before your own. In a word, it means submission.

If denying self speaks to our wills, taking up our cross speaks to our actions that follow. And although we don't carry literal wooden crosses, Jesus' metaphor still demands a literal application of the struggle God calls us each to bear. My cross—and your cross—represents the difficult obedience God requires daily.

Whenever someone took up a cross in Jesus' day, that person was not coming back. Taking up our cross daily represents what the apostle Paul would later describe as offering our bodies as a *living* sacrifice. This death to self can only happen as we renew our minds or, to use Jesus' words, as we set our minds on God's interests rather than man's (see Rom. 12:1-3; Phil. 2:3-11; 4:8; Col. 3:1-10).

Christ doesn't ask for volunteers to carry crosses for extra credit. A cross comes to "*anyone*" who follows Jesus. No exceptions. No alternatives. You are fastened to your cross. And like Jesus who bore the cross before us—and *for* us—the pain brings about God's glory and our good. Yes, our good (see Gal. 5:24).

Notice also the order of events: Jesus went to the cross *before* He experienced the joys of glory. When will we learn that it can be no different for us? When will we quit looking at the hardships in life as if we shouldn't have them?

Like Peter, our knee-jerk reaction demands heaven here and now. We expect marriages without struggle, bank balances in the black, well-balanced and obedient children, peace among our peers, and freedom from the incessant temptations of the flesh. We want God to meet our expectations of Him rather than our meeting His expectations of us.

In short, we don't want the cross, thank you very much.

My uncle has a painting hanging in his home. The picture shows a crusty old cowboy, rugged and wrinkled, squinting just past you. The caption at the bottom reveals his thoughts in simple terms: "There were a helluva lot of things they didn't tell me when I hired on with this outfit." That cowboy might as well be Peter or John or any of the other disciples. Or he could be you or me.

We had no idea what following Christ would demand when we started out. We *thought* we knew. We thought the Christian life meant that once we believed in Jesus, if we walked obediently, God would bless us, protect us, put us at ease—basically dote on us as His children. To some extent, we still expect that. But God wants to give us something greater than those things: He wants Christlikeness.

Once Jesus set straight a crowd who intended to make Him king by force, and He spoke some hard words. Afterwards, many no longer followed Him (see John 6:66). Jesus turned to His men with a question: "You do not want to leave too, do you?" (John 6:67, *NIV*).

Peter's answer reflects the attitude we should have: "Lord, to whom shall we go? You have the words of eternal life" (John 6:68, *NIV*). Jesus' words are hard words—but there are no alternatives. There cannot be.

Hardship is *normal* for the Christian life. Peter would later write, "Do not be surprised at the fiery ordeal among you, which comes upon you for your testing, as though some strange thing were happening to you" (1 Pet. 4:12). God promises struggles because God shapes us through them. Our growth comes no other way.

But mull this over as well: Our brief, little life here on Earth represents the *only* time in all of eternity when we can glorify God in the midst of struggle. Have you ever considered struggle as a temporary privilege? (Take the time to read the scene leading up to Acts 5:41.)

In heaven, we'll honor Christ to His face. But now we have the privilege of honoring Him in the face of struggle—by faith, not by sight. *Then* we'll glory in His transfiguration. *Now* we glorify Him beneath the cross we bear . . . and in temptation and weakness (see 2 Cor. 12:7-9). What a privilege!

I'm no masochist, believe me. But I'm eager to honor God during the longest life He will allow me and, while I'm here, to struggle well.

The Lord spent the next few months drilling into His men the coming cross and their need to surrender their wills. But their reaction to His words came as grief, fear, denial and misunderstanding (see Matt. 17:22-23; Mark 9:31-32; Luke 9:43-45). They still saw Jesus' mission through the fog of their own expectations. They still saw their primary pursuit as greatness and glory.

Glory would come, to be sure . . . but only through the cross. As much as they wouldn't want to, it was time to head that way.

To Jerusalem.

93

Note

1. *Merriam-Webster's Collegiate Dictionary,* 11th ed., s.v. "metamorphosis."

CHAPTER FIVE

WHAT DO YOU WANT FROM GOD?

And Jesus stopped and called them, and said,
"What do you want Me to do for you?"
MATTHEW 20:32

Jesus could have ridden our bus that day.

As we headed south from Galilee for Jerusalem, we couldn't travel the direct route through Samaria because of the delicate political situation in Palestinian towns like Ramallah and Nablus. Years before when I had visited Jacob's well near Nablus, the political climate was calm. But a shift in the wind blew the doors closed to the Jews—and to tourists. I've heard of busses with Israeli license plates getting stoned there! (That law is somewhere in Leviticus, I guess.) So we detoured east toward Beth-shan and the Jordan Rift Valley and turned south from there.

Jesus made a similar detour for similar reasons on His final trip to Jerusalem. After He had raised Lazarus in Bethany, the Sanhedrin plotted to kill Him. So Jesus withdrew from the Jerusalem area and went north to the village of Ephraim, probably modern et-Taiyiba (Old Testament Ophrah), a town on the edge of the Judean wilderness. Continuing north from Ephraim, Jesus would have spent His final days in Galilee before heading back to Jerusalem for His last Passover.

But instead of traveling back the direct route south through Samaria, He had to pass east along the border between Samaria and Galilee (see Luke 17:11). What for? Probably because the political and social situation blew the doors closed to the Jews. Just as it happened to us on our trip to Jerusalem.

This wasn't the first time the Samaritans refused Jesus passage through their land (an irony, in light of His acceptance there at the start of His ministry). Some months earlier, He had tried to go through to attend a Jerusalem feast, but the Samaritans had rebuffed Him (see Luke 9:51-56). As a result, Jesus and His disgruntled disciples had to go the long way around the barn . . . and I mean the *long* way.

This "road closed" sign through Samaria was all James and John could stand. In a fit of anger they roared, "Lord, do You want us to command fire to come down from heaven and consume them?" (v. 54). Now there's compassion for you. James and John must have had their quiet time that morning reading from 2 Kings 1:10-12, where we read that Elijah—whom they had recently seen at the transfiguration—called down fire from heaven to consume his enemies while also in Samaria. Kind of a sequel to the Mount Carmel barbecue (see 1 Kings 18:16-40). Somehow I think the brothers missed the application of that passage. Jesus thought so too and offered a quick rebuke. He nick-named James and John "Sons of Thunder" (Mark 3:17). How would you like for God to name you what you ask for?

But I can appreciate their aggravation. Because of today's political disputes and racial squabbles, I haven't been able to visit the region of Samaria for over eight years. What biblical sites does this include (or rather, *exclude*)? Heavyweights like Gibeah, Ramah, Bethel, Geba, Michmash, Shiloh, Shechem and the city of Samaria—just to name a few. Many of these sites lie in or near the strategic area of the tribe of Benjamin, called the "Central Benjamin Plateau." One estimate reveals that close to half of all Old Testament narratives occurred in this area. *Half of all Old Testament narratives*—and I can't see these places! Kind of makes you want to call down fire from heaven, doesn't it?

While my disappointment came with not being able to see a few key biblical sites, James and John's disappointment came from seeing way too many. This little detour of theirs more than doubled the length of their trip. And it also turned up the thermostat. Having to walk down into the Jordan Rift Valley, a drop in elevation of close to 4,000 feet, not only made their ears pop but also made their trip about 20 degrees hotter. In late March, they traded a nice three- or four-day trip at around 65 degrees on a well-traveled, fairly even road, for a trudge over some of the roughest, steepest terrain in Israel with temperatures in the mid to high 80s—and no shade.

When I hiked through this area one spring, the temperatures spiked well over 100 degrees. My Australian straw hat and the lukewarm water in my CamelBak did little to ease the discomfort. *How can the sun be hotter if I'm farther away from it?* Only the years of north Texas summers prepared me for the blistering temperatures that bounced off the rocks.

So Jesus could have ridden our bus that day. And if He had, I would have seen the disciples pouting in the back with their arms folded as we circumvented Samaria. *What good is glory and power without justice?* they'd be thinking. *Those Samaritans shouldn't have snubbed the Messiah! And what about Jesus? His passivity is embarrassing. His statement up north about His death made no sense, especially considering the glory of His transfiguration! I wish He'd make up His mind.*

Death, mercy, sacrifice, humility—these traits didn't fit the disciples' expectations of Jesus (and certainly not of themselves). The truths Jesus offered them ricocheted off their grand visions like heat off the hot rocks around them. They ignored the lessons.

But Jesus wouldn't let them do so for long.

As Jesus and His men straddled the border between Samaria and Galilee, their detour brought them to a village, perhaps Ginea (modern Jenin), where 10 lepers begged from a distance, "Jesus, Master, have mercy on us!" (Luke 17:13). These lepers, instead of hollering the usual "Unclean!" cried out to Jesus the Greek word *eliesos,* "mercy." This term solicited Jesus for more than sympathetic feelings. They cried for healing.

Jesus told these outcasts to go show themselves to the priests, as the Mosaic Law required for cured lepers. And *as they went,* they were healed (see Luke 17:14). (A great lesson in obeying before you see any benefits of obedience.) But Jesus made sure to point out to His men that while He healed all 10, only one returned to thank Him. And this one—get this—*was a Samaritan.* Perhaps coincidentally, today the city of Jenin holds a large Christian Arab community.

Think of it. Along the hostile border between Jews and Samaritans, this group of nine Jews and one Samaritan united around a common struggle—their disease. Somehow all the social and geopolitical lines between them vanished. But as soon as their common struggle disappeared, so did their commonality. And only the foreigner came back to say thanks.

Jesus was thanked only by the Samaritan—one of those the Sons of Thunder had wanted to toast.

—⁊⁊⁊—

On my very first trip to the Middle East, the group my wife and I were traveling with crossed over the Jordan River from Israel into the country of Jordan—a.k.a. "the Hashemite Kingdom of Jordan." It looked much the same on both sides of the river: same terrain, same blistering sun and same need for bottled water. But two different worlds entirely.

Even during a time of peaceful negotiations with Israel, Jordan required our entire bus to empty (of luggage and all) and for us to carry our luggage across the border to board a Jordanian bus. (I remember crossing the American/Canadian border once without even getting out of the car!) Giving your passport away to a total stranger for over half an hour can be unnerving. I became very familiar with the face of my watch. I felt even more nervous when everyone got their passport back except my wife! Turns out, our new Jordanian guide had taken it as a joke. *A joke? Is it okay to laugh?* After an hour of waiting at the border, we finally loaded our luggage, boarded the new bus and entered a new culture . . . and a surprising conversation.

As Jesus continued His detour, He too crossed the Jordan River into Perea (modern Jordan) and then headed south. On the way, large crowds followed Him, including some inquisitive Pharisees bent on trapping Jesus in His words. "Is it lawful for a man to divorce his wife for any reason at all?" they asked (Matt. 19:3). Now there's a cheerful topic on the way to Passover.

Like Jesus, we crossed the Jordan River . . . and, like Jesus, this issue of divorce came up. Now understand, in Jordan only Jordanian guides can guide you. Our own Christian guide had a gag order. And instead of teaching us Christians the biblical significance of Jordan—which is rich and fascinating (and why we were there)—our guide passed the time by educating us on the particulars of modern Jordan-ian culture. For hours we endured one bit of trivia after another, but the detail that stood out in my mind was about divorce.

"In Jordan a man can divorce his wife simply by saying 'I divorce you' three times," the guide informed us. Then he pointed his finger in the air and demonstrated the procedure. "I divorce you. . . . (*long pause*) . . . I divorce you. . . . (*long pause*) . . . I divorce you." I glanced at the women on the bus. Every one of them stared blankly out the win-dows. *How degrading*, I thought. This manner of divorcing a wife re-minded me of a parent who counts to three so that a mischievous child will straighten up: "*One!* . . . (*long pause*) . . . *TWO!* . . ."

While the response from our sisters in Christ at that moment was to bite their tongues, this speech elicited another reaction from these ladies: gratitude. Gratitude that they live in a country where—even with all its faults—women are afforded a bit of dignity and equality. Gratitude that they worship a God—and traveled with men and husbands—who viewed women as worthy of honor as "a fellow heir of the grace of life" (1 Pet. 3:7).

We added nothing in response to our guide's blather. But Jesus' reaction was different: "What did Moses write?" He asked those in-quiring about divorce (see Mark 10:3). Their answer betrayed a selec-tive memory.

"Moses permitted a man to write a certificate of divorce and send her away," they answered, referring to Deuteronomy 24:1 (Mark 10:4). Well, there you have it . . . straight from Scripture. (We always quote the verses that fit our biases, don't we?)

Jesus' reply took them from Deuteronomy back a few books to Genesis. (Moses wrote Genesis, too.) Their concern had been about divorce. But Jesus got more fundamental, essentially asking, "Rather, what about *marriage*?" (see Mark 10:6-9). Jesus took them to God's original intent as the standard, not to God's concession for hard hearts. "What therefore God has joined together," Jesus replied, "let no man separate" (Mark 10:9; see also Gen. 2:24).

As I think back to the miles we covered in that bus as it went rumbling down the highway in Jordan, I can't help but remember how out of place our guide's talk on divorce felt to us all. Here we came for a spiritual pilgrimage, and instead we endured the conventions of a chauvinistic culture. I wonder if the disciples got a similar feeling about the Pharisees' question on divorce as they journeyed south for the Passover. It must have seemed way out of context. Actually, though, it came as a perfect setup and example for what they needed to hear next—what they needed to hear most.

For the third time now, Jesus took His disciples aside and told them of His approaching death in Jerusalem. And all of what Jesus predicted would occur in just over a week. His words, however, fell on deaf ears. Luke would later write how absolutely clueless these men were about what Jesus had explained (see Luke 18:34). When Jesus finished, James and John pulled their fingers from their ears and approached Him with a request.

"Teacher, we want You to do for us whatever we ask of You."

"What do you want Me to do for you?" (Remember this question.)

"Grant that we may sit, one on Your right and one on Your left, in Your glory" (Mark 10:35-37).

Unbelievable! The Sons of Thunder asked the Son of God for the best seats in the house. Matthew tells us that, actually, the brothers got their *mother* to ask Jesus for them (see Matt. 20:20)! And if the tradition holds true that James and John were Jesus' cousins, the brothers used a family connection to influence Jesus' reply. *Who's going to say no to Aunt Salome, right?*

As I picture these men walking with Jesus, I wonder how long Jesus paused before His response. I wonder if—because it's quite possible geographically—at that moment they passed the place where the Jabbok River drains into the Jordan. They couldn't have missed the sight—a huge gorge cut by the Jabbok, large and stunning still today. Here, just a few miles upstream some 2,000 years earlier, a weary Jacob wrestled with the angel of the Lord for who would control Jacob's life. And if the angel of the Lord was, as some scholars believe, the pre-incarnate Christ, the memory would have held special significance for the Savior as James and John also began to wrestle for control with their request for power. With Jacob, the Lord had to wrench the patriarch's hip from

WALKING IN THE FOOTSTEPS OF JESUS

its socket before He would bless him (see Gen. 32:22-32). With the disciples, the lesson would come no easier. Perhaps they walked a short distance without a word between them. Finally, Jesus spoke.

"You do not know what you are asking. Are you able to drink the cup that I drink, or to be baptized with the baptism with which I am baptized?" (see Mark 10:38). In other words, Jesus asked them, "Can you suffer what I'm about to suffer—the death I just described to you—to sit where I will sit?"

"We are able," they blathered (v. 39).

I searched the book of Mark and found a startling fact: The only other time two individuals are placed to Jesus' right and left is when Jesus hung on the cross between two thieves (see Mark 15:27).

Jesus went on to tell these impulsive brothers that they would indeed suffer as He would suffer (see Matt. 20:23; Mark 10:39). And in a strange twist of historic irony, if we lined up all of Christ's faithful disciples facing us in the order of their deaths, to the far left would stand James and to the far right, John—the first and last apostles to die. But their request on the way to Jerusalem wasn't for a glorious death. It was for just plain glory.

Of course, when the other 10 disciples heard what the brothers asked, they fumed. Mark says they "began to feel indignant with James and John" (Mark 10:41). That means they got ticked that they didn't think of it first! *Why didn't I bring my mother on this trip?*

Picture this for a moment: Here we have Jesus facing death in Jerusalem, and these men are quibbling over who gets the box seats in the kingdom of God. What a contrast. What a shame.

Jesus stopped the trail ride and took advantage of a teachable moment. He brought them near and reminded them that the Gentiles—or unbelievers—use their authority as an opportunity for power. "But," Jesus charged—and the contrast in the original language reads strong—"it is *not* this way among you, but whoever wishes to become great among you shall be your servant" (Mark 10:43, emphasis added; see also Matt. 20:26).

It makes sense now how the subject of marriage fit in this context of abuse of power. Even today in the Middle East—as I saw so clearly—many men lord their authority over their wives with their fingers in the air: "I divorce you. . . . I divorce you. . . . I divorce you." Jesus' conversation with the Pharisees and His correction of the disciples illustrate this principle: God never gives authority as an opportunity for glory and power but as a responsibility to serve.

Paul's command for husbands to love their wives as Christ loves the Church means that the husband lays down his life for his wife . . . daily (see Eph. 5:22-33). What a far cry from the sanctioned chauvinism I saw that day on the bus. What a contrast from the life Christ modeled before His men.

I once heard someone flip the words of the *Westminster Shorter Catechism* to say, "The chief end of man is to glorify man and enjoy himself forever." The disciples had taken the world's abuse of power as their model. Many still do. Jesus offered a better model—Himself. His next words drove this home: "For even the Son of Man did not come to be served, but to serve, and to give His life a ransom for many" (Mark 10:45). Jesus' words in this key verse for the book of Mark reveal the key lesson the disciples needed to learn. Not the application for marriage per se, but the principle of position as a responsibility to serve—applied to *every* area of life. If anyone could rightly "lord it over" others, it would be the Lord. But Jesus refused to do that. Instead, He served.

The disciples would have to experience Jesus' death and resurrection before they would understand this lesson. And as they approached Jericho in the haze ahead, they were about to turn west toward Jerusalem—and toward the most difficult few days of their lives.

As our motor coach approached the outskirts of Jericho, the restlessness of our group became hard to contain. Hours of traveling south in the Jordan Rift Valley offered us little to look at . . . with only one bathroom break. I guess we could have stopped like the travelers of old and ducked into one of the caves dug into the valley walls. If we had, maybe we would have stumbled onto more finds like Qumran's

Dead Sea Scrolls in the caves just a few miles south. But if we had, we would have missed the ice cream. And the camel.

When you imagine an oasis, you could picture Jericho. Date palm trees clump together like coatless people on a chilly day. A green dot on a monochrome landscape, Jericho, "the city of palm trees," has a name that suggests a source of fresh water, which turned a wasteland into a garden (Deut. 34:3). Probably the oldest city in history, Jericho (Tel es-Sultan) is also the lowest city on Earth—800 feet below sea level. The underground spring that flows beside Old Testament Jericho's tell provided water for a marvelous irrigation system that distributed the life-giving supply to the perimeters of the plain—and to every single traveler who passed. On one occasion, Elisha purified this spring (see 2 Kings 2:21).

Any Sunday School child can tell you Jericho's most legendary event—the day its walls came tumbling down (see Josh. 6). When Joshua and the new nation of Israel crossed the Jordan River from the east, only Jericho stood between them and the Promised Land. Archaeology has revealed that the walls fell outward, allowing the Hebrews to climb over them and take the city. Today the tell of Old Testament Jericho—an archaeologist's paradise—sits as a 10-acre mound, only about as big as 2 city blocks, with over 26 separate layers of occupation beneath its topsoil.

As I exited the door of the air-conditioned bus, the hot air north of the Dead Sea hit me like a wall. The rustic tourist trap we stopped at capitalized on the heat by offering every possible flavor of soft drink and ice cream. And after visiting the restrooms, we were happy to oblige. As we slurped sodas and lapped ice creams, we waited on the stragglers by engaging in a humorous diversion: riding a camel.

Each time we stop at this place, I'm wielding a camera, so I have yet to ride the stinking beast. Maybe I should come clean: I grab the camera so that I don't have to ride! The experience looks like riding "Gilley's" electronic bull in Pasadena, Texas—hilarious and utterly humiliating. And pricey.

"Eight dollars," the Arab holding the camel quoted me in perfect English (I paid about as much for my cola and ice cream). But with my daughters eager, we forked over the cash. Clinging to carpets strapped on as a makeshift saddle, the girls hung on as the beige beast got up rear first, hurling them forward and tilting the horizon to 45 degrees. The owner began leading the camel on a brief lap around the parking lot with my daughters, now six feet higher, hanging on with all four limbs. As I watched what looked like riding the swells of the ocean, I marveled at God's design of this remarkable animal.

In a land where water is life, the camel was like driving a hybrid: You surrendered speed, style and acceleration for economy. Camel humps bulge with fat, which allows them to live without food for a time. (I wish the same was true of our bulges.) Even with all its draw-backs—including biting, spitting, stubbornness, odor and ugliness—the camel was the transportation of choice in biblical times. It could travel farther on less water than any other beast of burden.

Just looking at the animal proves God's sense of humor. In fact, Jesus once used the camel to highlight the humor and hypocrisy of people who nitpick holiness in small areas of life but neglect holiness where it counts, such as "justice and mercy and faithfulness." Jesus demanded, "These are the things you should have done without ne-glecting the others. You blind guides, who strain out a gnat and swal-low a camel!" (Matt. 23:23-24).

The hyperbole hits me square between the eyes as I consider how often I strain out the gnats of foul language but still manage to choke down the camels of bitterness and unforgiveness toward those who offend me (see Mic. 6:8). Sometimes the truth comes hard to swallow.

As the owner returned the smelly monster and my eager-to-dismount daughters, I figured he could have made at least 10 dollars if he charged us to dismount the camel instead of getting on.

By the time Jesus and His disciples strolled into New Testa-ment Jericho, the city sat at a distance from the Jericho of the Old Testament. And between these two sites sat some blind beggars who panhandled the pilgrims bound for Jerusalem. (The two cities, sitting side by side with the same name, explain why differ-ent Gospel accounts refer to Jesus meeting the blind men as He *left* Jericho and others express the event occurring as He *entered* [see

Matt. 20:29; Mark 10:46; Luke 18:35]. The geography resolves the apparent contradiction.)

When the blind man named Bartimaeus heard that Jesus was passing, He shouted again and again, "Jesus, Son of David, have mercy on me!" (Mark 10:47-48).

Notice Jesus' response, because He's asked this question before: "What do you want Me to do for you?" (Mark 10:51) *Remember this question?* Jesus had asked it of the disciples in response to *their* request (see v. 36). Mark intended that we should notice this.

In fact, Bartimaeus bookends a section that began with another blind man. In our journey to Bethsaida (see chapter 4), where Jesus healed the blind man, He had asked His disciples: "Do you not yet see or understand? Do you have a hardened heart? 'Having eyes, do you not see?'" (Mark 8:17-18).

Jesus then gave the Bethsaida blind man sight in stages, to reveal the disciples' partial understanding of Jesus. And every time Jesus tried to open their eyes and mention the cross, the disciples slammed their eyelids shut and groped for the Kingdom—and their own glorious places in it.

"What do you want Me to do for you?"

I wonder if Jesus looked at James and John as He asked blind Bartimaeus this question. And I wonder if James and John looked at each other when Bartimaeus gave his insightful reply: "Rabboni, I want to regain my sight!" (Mark 10:51). Seems an obvious answer, sure, but to the Sons of Thunder—and to all the glory-bound disciples—it should have pierced their hearts. When Jesus had asked them the same question earlier that day, they had requested glory. But Bartimaeus requested mercy. They had no perceived need for greater insight. But Bartimaeus requested to see. Those blinded by ambition had seen their greatest need as glory, and the one who knew he was blind saw his greatest need as mercy. The contrast was stark. You'd have to be blind to miss it.

The blind man's appeal should have pierced their hearts, but it didn't. It would take the harsh reality of the cross to peel the scales off the disciples' eyes, to reveal their misplaced ambition and false expectations, and to help them see Jesus for *all* of who He really is.

I polished off my soda at about the time our bus turned into the afternoon sun. Squinting, I scanned the western horizon for a familiar shape, a hill I had stood on years earlier to overlook the Jericho valley. Finally, I saw it: a lone peak in the distance.

"Isn't that Kypros?" I asked the driver.

"*Ken*" ("yes").

From that high and glorious vantage years prior, I had seen the entire Jericho valley, the Jordan River, the Dead Sea and the footpath Jesus started up that day from Jericho toward Jerusalem. Turning around in the opposite direction, I spotted the three towers atop the Mount of Olives beside Jerusalem—Jesus' final destination—with 18 miles of wilderness between us.

Leaving Jericho, Jesus began His ascent into the hill country of Judea by starting up the Wadi Qelt, a long gorge that drains the hills around Jerusalem eastward into the Jordan Rift Valley. Here Jesus would have passed between Herod the Great's palace buildings, which the late monarch built for himself in Jericho so that he had a place to escape Jerusalem's winters. The huge complex boasted large bathhouses, accessible through a vast reception hall, complete with mosaics, frescos, and gold and marble columns. The opulent palace straddled the ancient road Jesus traveled and connected to itself across a bridge that spanned the road. The buildings must have seemed striking to all who passed below—especially to disciples impressed with Herod's handiwork (see Mark 13:1).

When Jesus passed beneath the bridge between the buildings of Herod the Great, He must have considered this paranoid king who tried to kill Him as a boy—but who instead succeeded in slaughtering all baby boys in Bethlehem. Ironically, King Herod died in this palace while the true King of Israel lived to pass between its walls on His way to lay down His life. From my vantage atop Kypros, I could easily see the palace, which today lies in ruins—a testimony to all earthly glory.

As the road began to rise and more of the distance came into view, perhaps Jesus stood still as I did and looked in both directions. I could almost see Him, about a week now before His death, gazing back across the plains at the historical transitions that took place there. Right there, before where He stood. Right there, before where I stood.

High on the eastern hills opposite us, an old Moses overlooked the Promised Land, just before *he* died. Halfway between the two sets of hills lay a long valley with a line of green snaking southward through its center. The Jordan River began up north at the base of Mount Hermon, where Jesus first taught His disciples about His death and resurrection. The river ends here, just below Jericho, where it empties into the Dead Sea.

Here the river not only had its waters parted for Joshua to cross over; but at this same spot, centuries later, the river parted for Elisha to reenter the land after Elijah rode his chariot of fire into heaven. And as Jesus began His ministry, John the Baptist baptized Him here as the *heavens* parted. From Moses to Joshua . . . from Elijah to Elisha . . . and from John to Jesus—each of these great transitions near Jericho preceded the loss of a great life: Moses, Elijah and John. And now Jesus would pass the mantle on to His disciples after *His* death, resurrection and ascension.

The area had always been a place of transitions . . . from wandering to settling for Israel . . . from sin to salvation for Rahab and Zaccheus . . . from blindness to sight for Bartimaeus. But every place of new beginnings also requires endings, a change of heart and mind—the same repentance John cried out for when he baptized in the Jordan. The same repentance Jesus required when He preached to a nation bent on political freedom. This same change of heart Jesus calls for today.

The road beneath Jesus' feet left the bottom of the Wadi Qelt as its walls steepened, and the path wound its way along the southern ridge of the ravine. Today, a short walk up the path reveals Saint George's Monastery, which clings like a barnacle to the northern face of the wadi's cliffs. Housing one of the oldest monastic communities in Israel, the monastery has been inhabited since the fifth century and gives a vivid illustration of the ascetic lifestyle the wilderness has supported for thousands of years.

As I scanned the monastery's blue domes and white arches that dot the colorless canvas of the wilderness, I marveled at the time and ingenuity it would have taken to build and rebuild these structures. *Why would* anyone *choose to live way out here?* A friend of mine wondered if the monks in the monastery thought the same thing about us. I then realized that in my question lay the answer.

The remoteness of the Judean Wilderness offers an ideal hideaway for the recluse. It makes sense that throughout the Scriptures, this wilderness is often described as a place both of escape and of spiritual solitude; no one would want to follow. And because the wilderness sits today almost completely unchanged, I found it easy—even eerie—to gaze out and ponder that the likes of David, Jeremiah, John the Baptist and Jesus saw these hills almost exactly as I was seeing them.

As Jesus walked along, the path would have evoked memories of the weeks He had spent alone in this wilderness three and a half years earlier. After His baptism in the Jordan River, the Holy Spirit immediately led Jesus up into the solitude of this wilderness. Under searing heat and with scant springs of water available, Jesus wandered alone from the shade of one rock to another for 40 days. Then, after Jesus was hungry and weary, Satan approached Him with temptations that only the Son of God could have resisted. Jesus stood victorious by clinging to the words of Deuteronomy—the Scriptures Moses had penned in the Plains of Moab just east of there. And when Jesus emerged the victor, Satan left Him "until an opportune time" (see Luke 4:13). That opportune time lay ahead in Jerusalem.

The bus jerked slightly as the driver downshifted and we began our long climb through the Judean hills toward Jerusalem, still over 15 miles away. This journey from Jericho to Jerusalem would have been a tough hike. Walking uphill almost 3,500 feet in elevation, over a relatively short distance—ears popping, brow sweating, heart pounding—is when the disciples would have renewed their gripes about taking the long way.

I have a friend who lived in Israel a long time and recently hiked the very road Jesus walked from Jericho to Jerusalem. I envy him. He told me, though, that he would never attempt the rugged journey without a good map, plenty of water and many companions. This road was known as the "Ascent of Adummim," meaning "ascent of the red places," probably because of the red rocks there. In the third century, Eusebius identified the road with the village called Maledonmnei, or Tal`at ed-Damm—"ascent of blood." The Latin name for the city refers to it as the "ascent of bloodstains," probably because of the blood spilled there by thieves. Even today, my friend told me, Bedouins of shady character dwell in and among the hills, and traveling alone is foolhardy.

For this reason, Jesus used the Ascent of Adummim as the setting for His parable of the "good Samaritan," a complete oxymoron to the first-century Jew—everyone knew that Samaritans weren't "good." In Jesus' parable, the man who fell among thieves lay ignored by two elite Jews—a priest and a Levite—and only the detested Samaritan stopped to help. *Only the Samaritan.*

And only the Samaritan leper returned to thank Jesus, too. Remember?

The disciples didn't. They just remembered that the Samaritans caused this difficult detour to begin with. They forgot the Samaritan leper's gratitude, and the Samaritan woman's repentance, and the parable of the good Samaritan's mercy along the very road they walked. They also forgot Jesus' rebuke of their misplaced anger. The very ones James and John wanted to toast modeled Jesus' example of sacrifice better than they did.

Today, the "Inn of the Good Samaritan"—a once crumbling, now renovated structure commemorating Jesus' story—sits on the modern road our bus strained to climb, some distance south of the true road Jesus walked. The building reminded me of the parable and the disciples' complete blindness to Jesus' mission.

Jesus didn't come as their ticket to glory. He came to seek and to save and to make fishermen fishers of men. But in their tunnel vision for glory, the disciples stumbled over every speed bump Jesus put in their path.

After our motor coach groaned past the road sign that read "Sea Level," I remembered that our steady ascent had brought us up about 800 feet from Jericho—with over 2,500 more to climb to Jerusalem. On pilgrimages to Passover and other feasts, Jews would "go up to Jerusalem" and sing the Psalms of Ascents as they traveled. This group of songs from the Psalter (Psalms 120–134) we could compare to our Christmas carols. They were sung on holidays (or holy days), everyone knew the words, and they stirred up critical reminders of basic themes in a believer's life: faith, forgiveness, family, children, peace, brotherhood, sacrifice and right attitudes toward God and others.

But just as the Christmas carols ring out today during December in shopping malls (I call them "mauls") full of frenzied, materialistic consumers, so many who ascended to Jerusalem with Jesus that day sang the Psalms of Ascents with their lips alone. In fact, among Jesus and His disciples, I believe only Jesus sang with His heart fully engaged.

What a bit of tangled emotions He must have felt. He had already experienced the rejection of His family and His nation in Galilee. And as Jesus saw the ridge of the Mount of Olives in the distance, He knew more rejection lay just beyond it—the rejection of His offering the kingdom to Israel. He knew He would be crucified in Jerusalem. He had predicted it.

Jesus may have remembered a barefoot King David who ascended the Mount of Olives in his flight from Absalom, fleeing down the very road Jesus was walking up. King David fled Jerusalem among a hail of hurled stones to avoid a clash that would cost his son Absalom his life (see 2 Sam. 15:30–16:14). But Jesus, the rejected King of Israel, the Son of David, instead faced the inevitable conflict—*knowing* it would cost His life—to save a people who would either reject Him or use Him as their fast pass to glory.

Jesus asked one question that day: "What do you want Me to do for you?" One question that received *two* completely different responses. His disciples answered, "I want glory!" Bartimaeus responded, "I want mercy!"

Now point the question at yourself. If Jesus came up to you right now and asked, "What do you want Me to do for you?" how would you answer? What do *you* want from God?

Not sure? Perhaps we should ask it another way: "What do you *ask* God for?"

Some of us ask God to make our life easier. Others of us think we need God to make us more like Him. For most, it's a blurred bit of both. But when we can't have both, to which side do our prayers default? It all shakes down to this: Whatever we ask God for reveals our perception of need. And like the disciples, we often only perceive our need for relief, ease and promotion.

Did Jesus promise His disciples great places in the Kingdom? Absolutely. But the road to getting to those great places led straight to the cross. The disciples did all they could to avoid this reality. And so do we.

Great transitions in our lives often come as a result of great pain. Perhaps we endure the death of a loved one, a mentor or a dream. Sometimes the unexpected loss of our job, our health or even our marriage comes as an unwelcome course in the curriculum God has for us. Often when we see the quickest and easiest way to where we want to go—or even where we should go—God allows Samaritans to cut across our path and force us to take a longer—and harder—route.

But Jesus never just points the way and says, "See you there." He walks with us through these course corrections. In fact, He *leads us* through them. Our problem? We want Jesus to lead the way *we* want to go. We want the easy walk to Jerusalem. We want the short track to heaven on Earth. We want glory. But Jesus wants more for us.

Jesus wants our holiness first and foremost. His destination for us is transformation, not just glorification. And He loves us enough to lead us along a path of struggle, if that's what it takes to get us from here to there. Even for Christ, the road to glory included the cross. Why should we expect any less for we who follow Jesus (see Rom. 8:17; Phil. 2:5-11)?

Even on our best days, we see as looking in a mirror dimly (much like Bethsaida's half-healed blind man). The scales fall from our eyes as we take up our cross and follow Him into the inevitable pain of faithfulness and sacrificial love (see 1 Cor. 13:12). With each step, we come closer to understanding the paradox of Jesus' words to His glory-bound followers: "For whoever wishes to save his life will lose it, but whoever loses his life for My sake and the gospel's will save it" (see Mark 8:35).

The blind men bookend this lesson, hemming us in like walls we cannot scale. We need mercy. We need the attitude that we live and die to *give* glory and not to *get* it. The glory belongs to God and is His for the giving—not ours for the asking.

Jesus takes us to the cross to show us what ambition has blinded us to: that our greatest need from Him isn't glory but mercy. Our greatest need from God isn't for Him to change our circumstances but for Him to use our circumstances to change *us*.

As our bus of weary travelers approached Jerusalem, I felt an eagerness I always feel when the ridge of the Mount of Olives comes into view—I know the Holy City lies on the other side. The first sight of Jerusalem never gets old to me. It must have been the same to the pilgrims who ascended the road that day with Jesus.

As Jesus and His disciples approached the ridge ahead, every heart pounded. The disciples could only see glory on the other side. *Their* glory—and Jesus was the ticket.

But Jesus saw the cross. He asks us to see the same.

CHAPTER SIX

JERUSALEM AT LAST!

"O Jerusalem, Jerusalem, the city that kills the prophets and stones those sent to her! How often I wanted to gather your children together, just as a hen gathers her brood under her wings, and you would not have it!"

LUKE 13:34

People often ask me if I have a favorite place I've visited in Israel.

"You mean other than Jerusalem?" I usually begin.

No other city in history comes close to Jerusalem's significance. Others have had more power, more land, more people, more natural resources—even more prestige—but none has more significance. And none ever will.

Yet when you see Jerusalem for the first time, you may wonder why all the fuss. Except for the Temple Mount with its golden Dome of the Rock, the city seems drab. No skyscrapers pierce the skyline of Israel's capital city. Only some scattered antennae, towers, domes, cranes, crosses and crescent moons protrude in a tangled mess—like wheat and tares. Myriads of dumpy buildings and uneven rooftops betray the hodgepodge of intentions each era has imposed on the city's fixed spaces.

Even the first-century Greek geographer Strabo saw Jerusalem as an undesirable place no one would fight for.[1] But remember, God has chosen the foolish, the weak, the base and the despised things of the world—that includes you and me—"so that no man may boast before God" (1 Cor. 1:28; see also vv. 27,29).

Instead of only businessmen and women with briefcases and Palm Pilots, you see plain-clothed Arabs, Orthodox Jews, armed teenage soldiers and a dozen tour busses all doing their best to avoid each other.

We pulled to a stop near a kneeling camel in the parking lot of the Seven Arches Hotel. Rather than stopping to lodge, we got out to look.

Here, on top of the Mount of Olives, I've found no better place to see Jerusalem's sprawling panorama. A deep sigh is appropriate. You can't take it all in without turning your head. We never stop here long enough.

As soon as we arrived, though, several postcard-peddling merchants tried to patter us a 10-pack bargain: "Only one dallah! One dallah!" I felt as if we had disturbed an ant bed. One peddler offered us a ride on his camel. Another wore 17 baseball caps stacked on his head, each a different color. ("I would have bought a hat if you had a blue one," I heard one passenger joke to the peddler. Big mistake. At a later stop, the peddler met him with a blue hat!)

As we overlooked the Old City, with its thick, ancient walls that enfold the Temple Mount, most of the cameras clicked in its direction. After a few minutes, nearly everyone seemed surprised to learn that the location of the original city of Jerusalem, the City of David, sits inconspicuously south of the Temple Mount on a mere 10 acres.

Flanked on two sides by steep valleys—the Kidron Valley on the east and the Central Valley on the west—the ancient City of David enjoyed a tremendous military advantage. Its easy defensibility gave the original inhabitants overconfidence when King David arrived to conquer the city, which was then called Jebus. "You shall not come in here, but the blind and lame will turn you away," the Jebusites told him, thinking, "David cannot enter here" (2 Sam. 5:6).

But David did conquer the city by entering up "through the water tunnel" (2 Sam. 5:8), probably the modern "Warren's Shaft." I have peered down this shaft. Only a very brave and capable man could have climbed it with a sword and a lamp; perhaps for this reason, David offered the role of general to the first man to go up and kill a Jebusite (see 1 Chron. 11:6).

Warren's Shaft descended to the major source of water for Jerusalem, the Gihon Spring. Unfortunately, the spring surfaced near the bottom of the slope by the Kidron Valley, a weak and vulnerable place from which to get water during a time of siege. King Hezekiah would later expand the city wall to include the Western Hill. (When I saw Hezekiah's "Broad Wall" in the Jewish Quarter, a cat sitting on the wall seemed as aware of the significance of the site as those who passed by.)

Hezekiah also plugged up the surface source of the Gihon and tunneled underneath the City of David to the Central Valley, allowing the flowing water to pool inside the walls (see 2 Chron. 32:30). This Pool of Siloam gave water to the ancient inhabitants and also gave stage to one of Christ's miracles (see John 9:7). Recent excavations have unearthed the steps surrounding this massive pool. Its size puts to shame the smaller Byzantine pool we originally attributed as Siloam, where I've seen little Palestinian boys swim in their underwear.

From the Mount of Olives where we stood, a keen eye can see specifics in the City of David. Near its summit, a stepped-stone structure, one of the largest Iron Age structures ever excavated, probably supported David's palace. From that vantage, David could easily have looked down over the homes built on the slope below him and seen Bathsheba bathing that fateful evening. The modern village of Silwan, just across the Kidron Valley from the City of David, has constructed its homes in a similar way. Near the Iron Age structure sits, of all things, an ancient stone toilet seat discovered in the ruins (I call it "David's throne").

With a squint I could see the building that covered the Gihon Spring, the site where Nathan and Zadok anointed Solomon to inherit the *real* throne of David. "Long live King Solomon!" David had them shout while his son Solomon rode on the back of David's mule (1 Kings 1:34).

I turned my gaze from the Gihon to my right, where Jesus had topped the Mount of Olives on the back of a donkey. Jesus' presentation of Himself on the animal fulfilled Zechariah's prophecy that Jerusalem's king would appear and bring salvation (see Zech. 9:9,16). A magnificent, panoramic view of the city and Temple spread before them. The crowds would have cheered, not unlike the shouts at Solomon's coronation.

"Hosanna to the Son of David; 'Blessed is He who comes in the name of the LORD'; Hosanna in the highest!" the crowds shouted (Matt. 21:9). "Blessed is . . . the King of Israel" (John 12:13). Their words originated in Psalm 118:25-26, which promised political freedom and prosperity from the Messiah. The crowd expected God's kingdom immediately (see Luke 19:11), in spite of the fact that Jesus had just taught them otherwise. "Hosanna" comes from the Hebrew *hoshi-ah nah* and means "Save us now, we beseech You!" The first word, *hoshi-ah*, stems from the same root as Jesus' name in Hebrew—*Yeshua*—and means "salvation" (see Matt. 1:21).

Jesus rode in on a donkey—a clear statement that He was the King. The crowd shouted (the disciples probably the loudest), "Blessed is He who comes in the name of the LORD!"—a clear statement that He was the King.

And the leadership of Israel? A predictable response: "Teacher, rebuke Your disciples," the Pharisees crabbed (Luke 19:39). In other words, they weren't buying any of it. Jesus countered that if His disciples ceased their praises, the rocks would shout. (A friend of mine says this would have been the first ever rock concert!)

Ironically, while the crowds shouted verses 25-26 from Psalm 118, no one shouted verse 22—the very verse the Pharisees were fulfilling. Jesus became "the stone which the builders rejected." The Lord Jesus knew the next few days would finalize Israel's rejection of Him. And Friday they would put the nails in the coffin.

As He made His way down the steep slope and the crowd continued their shouts of joy, Jesus saw Jerusalem and wept over it: "If you had known in this day, even you, the things which make for peace! But now they have been hidden from your eyes" (Luke 19:42).

"Something greater than Solomon is here," Jesus had announced in Galilee to the Pharisees who rejected Him (see Matt. 12:23-24,42). They wanted no part of Jesus as the "Son of David" (v. 23). They wanted a king like all the other nations.

It hardly seemed a "triumphal entry."

—⁓—

We began the sharp descent from the Mount of Olives by following a narrow road with high walls on either side. On top of the walls, colored pieces of broken glass jutted up from the concrete as a primitive barbed-wire fence. Immediately to my left was a sign: "Tombs of the Prophets Haggai, Zechariah and Malachi." Although the first-century *kokhim* (shaft) tombs could not have belonged to these sixth- and fifth-century B.C. prophets, I found it interesting that Zechariah, who foresaw Israel's King coming on a donkey, would allegedly rest on the slope where his words found fulfillment.

The high wall on my left overlooked a vast Jewish graveyard. Literally thousands of white tombs gave testimony to the hope that when the Messiah comes, "His feet will stand on the Mount of Olives," and those buried there will stand first in line for blessing (Zech. 14:4). Although the Messiah will raise all Jews from these graves, not every resurrection will rejoice in His presence (see Dan. 12:2; Rev. 20:11-15). Jesus' words to Nicodemus remain God's standard for entrance into His kingdom: "You must be born again." Strategic burial plots fail to impress God.

In contrast, the high wall to my right enclosed the grounds of the Dominus Flevit Church. The chapel and its name memorialize the moment "the Lord wept" over Jerusalem (see Luke 19:41).

I had to marvel at the contrast on either side of me. One wall guarded the hope that the Messiah *will come* one day. The other wall guarded the belief that He *already had come*—but was rejected. Only a narrow, steep road separates these two walls. But the distance between them is eternal.

We passed through the metal gate into the green, cultivated grounds surrounding the Dominus Flevit Church. The roof of the quaint chapel resembles the shape of an inverted teardrop. I entered and walked to the altar on the right and the large arced window that frames the city of Jerusalem. The window's decorative wrought-iron bars depict a cup, a loaf, thorns and a cross. A few potted plants and candles sat on the sill. The capstone above the window supports a stone relief of Jesus riding a donkey with His face in His hands.

I pondered the words of the weeping Messiah: "If you had known in *this day* . . ." (Luke 19:42, emphasis added).

The prophet Daniel penned a meticulous prediction of *the day* when the Messiah would appear in Jerusalem. Exactly 483 Jewish years—or 476 Gregorian years—from the rebuilding of Jerusalem in

March 444 B.C., "Messiah the Prince" would appear (Dan. 9:25).[2] If the Jewish leaders had taken seriously Daniel's challenge "to know and discern" the timing (v. 25), Jesus would have topped the hill as He did in March of A.D. 33 to see a banner draped over the walls of Jerusalem: "Welcome, Messiah!" But instead, they rebuked the notion.

A group of French tourists began singing outside the chapel. I heard their words but could only appreciate their melody. One recurring word I did recognize though: "Jerusalem."

As I stared out the window at the city over which the Lord had wept, it seemed as though I gazed through a porthole of time. The wrought-iron elements of Jesus' Passion overshadowed the city. I could not see Jerusalem without also seeing the cross. Neither could Jesus when He was here that day.

We circled Jerusalem and entered on the west, just opposite where Jesus went in. Inside the Jaffa Gate, I sat on a bench beside three middle-aged locals. One wore thick glasses on the end of his nose and read a Hebrew paper, while his body sporadically jerked from a niggling cough. The two wrinkled Jews beside him talked incessantly to each other; one never stopped smiling. Nearby, a man in a crisp, blue shirt looked distinguished until he laughed, revealing missing teeth.

These men reminded me of the elders who sat at the gates in biblical times and judged the cases of the land (see Ruth 4:1-12; Prov. 31:23). In Jesus' day, a gate stood here as well; I wondered how many cases judged here found justice. I glanced across David Street at the looming Citadel, where Pilate had judged Jesus. (More details about the Citadel in chapter 7.)

Jesus likely entered Jerusalem near what is today called Stephen's Gate, or Lion's Gate. He walked into the Temple and looked around—though the Gospel of Mark is silent about what Jesus saw (see Mark 11:11). Leaving the Temple, Jesus and His disciples crossed the Kidron Valley and scaled the Mount of Olives to spend the night with friends in Bethany.

We left the city walls via the Dung Gate and took the downhill sidewalk around into the Kidron Valley, near where Jesus crossed.

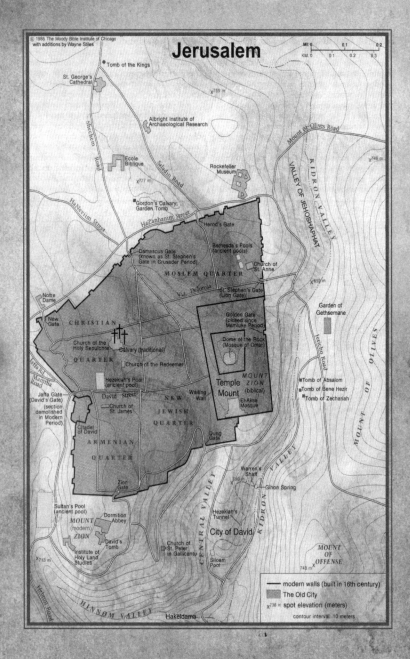

Jerusalem

© 1985 The Moody Bible Institute of Chicago
with additions by Wayne Stiles

MI. 0   0.1   0.2
KM. 0   0.1   0.2   0.3

Tomb of the Kings

St. George's Cathedral

Albright Institute of Archaeological Research

Ecole Biblique

Rockefeller Museum

MOUNT OF OLIVES ROAD

VALLEY OF JEHOSHAPHAT

KIDRON VALLEY

x746 m

Gordon's Calvary; Garden Tomb

HaNevi'im Street

HaZanhanim Street

Herod's Gate

Damascus Gate (known as St. Stephen's Gate in Crusader Period)

Bethesda's Pools (ancient pools)

Church of St. Anne

MOSLEM QUARTER

Via Dolorosa

St. Stephen's Gate (Lion Gate)

x699 m

Notre Dame

New Gate

CHRISTIAN

QUARTER

Church of the Holy Sepulchre

Calvary (traditional)

Church of the Redeemer

Hezekiah's Pool (ancient pool)

David Street

Golden Gate (closed since Mamluke Period)

Dome of the Rock (Mosque of Omar)

Garden of Gethsemane

MOUNT ZION (biblical)

Temple Mount

Tomb of Absalom

Tomb of Bene Hezir

Tomb of Zechariah

MOUNT OF OLIVES

Jericho Road

Jaffa Rd.

Mamilla Rd.

Jaffa Gate (David's Gate) (section demolished in Modern Period)

Citadel of David

Church of St. James

NEW JEWISH QUARTER

Wailing Wall

El-Aksa Mosque

ARMENIAN

QUARTER

Dung Gate

Zion Gate

Warren's Shaft

Gihon Spring

CENTRAL VALLEY

KIDRON VALLEY

Sultan's Pool (ancient pool)

MOUNT (modern) ZION

Dormition Abbey

David's Tomb

Institute of Holy Land Studies

x713 m

Church of St. Peter in Gallicantu

Hezekiah's Tunnel

City of David

Siloam Pool

MOUNT OF OFFENSE

x748 m

Hinnom Rd.

HINNOM VALLEY

Hakeldama

— modern walls (built in 16th century)

The Old City

x738 m spot elevation (meters)

contour interval: 10 meters

Thousands of Jewish graves cover the Mount of Olives, overlooking the Temple Mount in Jerusalem.

I passed two inimitable tombs, one with the shape of an upside-down funnel. Called "Absalom's Pillar," the stone structure takes its misnomer from the arrogant prince's act of erecting a monument to himself in the King's Valley (see 2 Sam. 18:18). The tomb dates to the first century, way after Absalom's time, and could have been brand new when Jesus crossed the Kidron.

I saw that the other mausoleum carries the name "Tomb of Zechariah," and I couldn't help but wonder, *How many tombs does Zechariah get?* A Hebrew inscription on the adjacent burial place linked it to the priestly family of Hezir (see 1 Chron. 24:15).

I saw an opening in one of the large tombs, and with the wonder of a boy, I entered. *What will I find? Ancient artifacts? Bones? Biblical inscriptions?* My eyes adjusted, but my nose could not. I felt idiotic for being so naïve. Someone had defecated in the tomb and dumped garbage everywhere. Disenchanted, I circled and left.

What Jesus found in the Temple that day was just as disappointing.

—⁓—

The cool Jerusalem morning bustled with activity. Outside my hotel window in the Christian Quarter, uniformed school children waited for their bus, laughing and chasing each other. Distant city traffic hummed outside the New Gate. Our group began to gather outside. I eagerly anticipated the day.

We walked down the streets called Casa Nova and Greek Orthodox Patriarchate and stopped at Christian Quarter Road. Beneath my feet, countless shoes had polished the bumpy cobblestones and slabs of limestone that comprised Jerusalem's pavement.

We turned the corner into the Ali Baba shop, a great place to get souvenirs, Dead Sea products, and a fair rate of exchange for shekels. (I had discovered that morning that just as there is no international standard for currency, so all hotel shower mechanisms seem to work in a way you've never seen before. If you accidentally activate the showerhead before you get the water temperature right, you may suddenly speak in tongues.)

While others finished exchanging money, I waited in the narrow, pedestrian-only road outside the shop. Barely 10 feet wide, the narrow road contained countless markets that spilled out into the open-air walkway. Awnings from either side met in the middle and shaded the merchants, merchandise and the throng that busied the literal labyrinth of crisscrossing passages and paths. I've walked these roads in the very early morning hours; the storefronts bear bolted metal doors that transform the usual busy streets into long, silent hallways.

I turned around toward the stone wall opposite the shop. It seemed difficult to realize that on the other side of the inconspicuous old stone wall stood the most significant spot in the city—or, I could say, the most significant spot in the universe. For behind the stones, within the Church of the Holy Sepulcher, is the site where Jesus died and rose again.

Merchants hocked crosses and paintings of Christ's agony near where it actually occurred. People passed the wall unaware. Or perhaps indifferent.

121

My musings cut short, our group reassembled and prepared to navigate the narrow, bustling street. We took a breath and dove into the gaggle of people.

The Christian Quarter seemed like a collision between faith and commerce. Here "marketing" finds its mother, and the term "bazaar" serves as an apt homonym to "bizarre." Lit with bare bulbs and buzzing fluorescents, most shops measured about 6 feet wide by 15 feet deep. Literally every inch had something to sell: sandals, Middle Eastern clothing, embroidered book bags, backpacks, chalices, necklaces, bracelets, earrings, jewelry boxes, menorahs, candles, prayer shawls, religious icons, rosary beads, crosses, olive wood, nativity sets, and Armenian dinner plates with painted scenes of Jerusalem.

One shop sold nothing but multicolored candies. Another, fruits, nuts and Mars candy bars. Red pomegranates the size of onions sat stacked in a pyramid. *Should I take one from the bottom?* I passed spice shops with ground curry, ginger, cinnamon, saffron, black pepper and a dozen other seasonings in uncovered plastic bowls. What wonderful colors and smells! And then there were the shops selling uncovered raw meat—with flies and not-so-wonderful smells.

Every face was a stranger—and some stranger than others. Most merchants wore a smile under their mustache and puffed a hookah pipe with dubious contents. Hands outstretched, the peddlers baited the passersby like lures on a trotline. One character was determined to get my attention.

"Excuse me, sir!"

"No, thank you." I maintained my pace.

"Sir! Excuse me, please!" He followed and held out a pack of postcards. "Look! Three dallah!"

"That's very nice. No, thank you."

"*One* dallah!" he countered. For some reason, every set of postcards bottoms out at one dollar. A friend of mine calls the Via Dolorosa the "Via One-Dollar-Rosa." I stopped, turned and looked the merchant dead in the eyes.

"No, thank you," I smiled. He shrugged and turned in one movement, beginning again with someone behind me.

Some tourists deserve the attention. They look so . . . well, touristy. I'm thinking of the typical retired gentleman with two cameras, dark shoes with knee-high socks, walking shorts, pasty legs, eyeglasses with flip-up shades, and a hat that looks like Gilligan's. Got the picture? He might as well wear a sign that says "Sell me something!"

In one shop, I saw a long, beautiful shofar, the horn from a ram. I asked the merchant if he would blow it. He took a deep breath and pressed his lips tightly on the tip, releasing a long blast followed by a half-dozen short ones. It sounded marvelous—and in Jerusalem!

"That's great!" I cheered.

"Sixty-five dallah," he quickly added.

Most of the Old City straddles the Central Valley, a simpler name for what Josephus called the Tyropoean Valley, or "Valley of the Cheesemakers." Accordingly, walking the slanted streets of Jerusalem requires climbing countless stairs. Anything with wheels, like carts and wheelbarrows, have to employ the makeshift ramps added to the steps—an obvious afterthought.

In Jesus' day, because the valley separated the Western Hill from the Temple Mount, a bridge spanned the gorge to allow easier passage for priests. Wilson's Arch, the massive bridge's support that I saw in the Western Wall Tunnel, rose 75 feet from the ground in Jesus' day. Today it supports part of the Muslim Quarter and covers a prayer room for Jewish men.

In most ways, the Jerusalem that Jesus entered was very different from the city I experienced. But in other ways, it wasn't.

When we read about the Lord entering the Temple the morning following His night in Bethany, we finally discover what He had seen the day before: a collision between faith and commerce. Money changers shortchanged the pilgrims; merchants sold "clean" animals that would have dunged up the Temple grounds, defiling God's place of worship (see Mark 11:12-18).

Jesus displayed His authority as Messiah by promptly cleaning house, just as He had done three years earlier (see John 2:14-16). He drove out those who used worship as an opportunity for financial gain—a charade the Lord still despises (see 1 Tim. 6:5).

"Is it not written," Jesus reminded them, " 'My house shall be called a house of prayer for all the nations'? But you have made it a 'robbers' den' " (Mark 11:17; cf. Isa. 56:7; Jer. 7:11). The phrase "robbers' den" comes from Jeremiah's rebuke to those who abused God's first Temple in the prophet's day. Jeremiah stood in the Temple and told the leaders to go to Shiloh and see what remained of the Tabernacle. Its ruins foreshadowed the destruction of the first Temple (see Jer. 7:12; 26:6). And Jesus quoting Jeremiah predicted the same grievous outcome for the second Temple.

Words and works like this did little to curry the favor of the Jewish leaders. Instead, they began looking for a way to kill Jesus (see Mark 11:18; Luke 19:47). Every day Jesus taught in the Temple, and steadily their anger toward Him swelled. Why? Because Light reveals what lurks in darkness (see John 1:5; 3:19-21; 8:12; Acts 26:15-18). Or, said less cryptically, because Jesus exposed their hypocrisy.

One of my favorite hole-in-the-wall places in Jerusalem sells cheap pizza and ice cream on a stick. Outside the café, umbrellas advertising cigarettes shade tables surrounded by colored plastic chairs. The seats give a great view of the goings-on in the Jewish Quarter. However, an adjacent café also lays claim to the tables—and loudly told us so during our visit! We cooled the dispute by purchasing pizza from both establishments.

An elderly Jew with a white beard shuffled down the street and in the distance pigeons lit on the Hurva Synagogue arch. A young Jewish woman chatted on her cell phone while an ultra-orthodox father led his two sons, one by each hand. A couple of little boys with backpacks and yarmulkes strode by where we sat.

I noticed a huge decorative millstone next to my table. Jesus' words came to mind: "Whoever causes one of these little ones who believe in Me to stumble, it would be better for him to have a heavy millstone hung around his neck, and to be drowned in the depth of the sea" (Matt. 18:6). I thought about those little boys who passed, who were learning a religion of deed, not creed. I wondered over whose neck the millstone would hang.

When Jesus entered the Temple after His triumphal entry, children began shouting what the disciples had proclaimed: "Hosanna to the Son of David" (Matt. 21:15). But when the self-appointed "God Squad" heard the shouts, they responded true to form: "Do You hear what these children are saying?" the indignant leaders needled Jesus (Matt. 21:15).

"Yes," Jesus responded. "Have you never read, 'Out of the mouth of infants and nursing babies You have prepared praise for Yourself'?" (Matt. 21:16). That had to have stung!

Jesus was suggesting that they hadn't read their Bibles, yet the scribes were reputed experts in Scripture. If they had read the verse, they would have known how it ends: "From the lips of children and infants you have ordained praise *because of your enemies, to silence the foe and the avenger*" (Ps. 8:2, *NIV,* emphasis added). Jesus implied that *they* were His enemies, whom God silenced with children. (Words like these would never make a chapter in *How to Win Friends and Influence People*.)

Jesus spoke parables to and against the religious leaders, teaching that He would offer the kingdom of God they had rejected to another generation of Jews who would receive it with repentance (see Matt. 21:28-46). Jesus again asked them, "Did you never read in the Scriptures?" and quoted the triumphal entry's missing verse from Psalm 118: "The stone which the builders rejected, this became the chief corner stone; this came about from the LORD, and it is marvelous in our eyes" (Matt. 21:42; cf. Ps. 118:22). Peter would later quote this verse when he faced the same council that condemned Christ (see Acts 4:11; 1 Pet. 2:7).

The religious leaders tried a number of times to trap Jesus in His words in order to have some reason to accuse Him. But Jesus saw through their duplicity and openly spoke against it (see Matt. 22:15-40; Mark 12:13-34).

"The teachers of the law and the Pharisees sit in Moses' seat," Jesus told the people, "so you must obey them and do everything they tell you" (Matt. 23:1-2, NIV). No doubt, the leaders nodded in agreement for the first time. "But do not do what they do," Jesus continued, "for they do not practice what they preach" (Matt. 23:3, NIV). Jesus then turned to the leaders themselves and fired both barrels: "Woe to you, teachers of the law and Pharisees, you hypocrites!"—a statement Jesus blasted word-for-word six times in one passage (Matt. 23:13,15, 23,25,27,29, NIV). The Greek term for "hypocrite" refers to stage actors who wear a mask. Also, Jesus pronounced them "a son of hell" (v. 15), "blind guides" (vv. 16,24), "whitewashed tombs" (v. 27), "serpents" (v. 33) and a "brood of vipers" (v. 33). Wow! Where's that millstone?

Jesus finished His slamming indictment by returning again to Psalm 118: "Behold, your house is being left to you desolate! For I say to you, from now on you will not see Me until you say, 'Blessed is He who comes in the name of the LORD!'" (Matt. 23:38-39; cf. Ps. 118:26). In other words, until the leadership of Israel recognizes Jesus as the Messiah, the physical kingdom of God on Earth will not come. "Until" speaks of a future salvation for Israel, which the Bible marvelously promises (see Rom. 11:25-29). They still have hope . . . but on that generation, the door was closing.

As Jesus left the Temple, His disciples pointed out the massive, beautiful stones and buildings.

"Do you see these great buildings?" Jesus answered, "Not one stone will be left upon another which will not be torn down" (Mark 13:2). They continued across the Kidron Valley to the Mount of Olives and overlooked the Temple Mount with the evening sun in their faces. There Jesus gave His "Olivet Discourse," further explaining the coming judgment on Jerusalem (see Matt. 24–25:46; Mark 13; Luke 21:5-36). In more than one way, the sun was setting on Israel.

I walked through a narrow passage with a wall to my left and a large fig tree to the right. One lone bird, screaming like a Texas sparrow, chirped its heart out. The pathway opened into a broad excavated area south of the Temple Mount. Alternating long and short steps, dating from the first century, slowed my approach as I ascended. At the top, I faced a bricked-up double gate. Above a jumble of other stones and a protruding arch, I could make out half of the lintel stone and relieving arch from a gate dating to the time of Christ. When people exited the Temple after worshipping, they exited through this gate. Jesus would have also exited here many times.

I turned around. The steps below me had been a place where Jesus would have taught the crowds. Here Gamaliel trained a young Saul, later to become the apostle Paul (see Acts 22:3). Here Peter preached to the crowds on the Day of Pentecost, baptizing thousands in the ritual baths, or *mikvot*, which I could see still next to the steps (see Acts 2:41).

I looked at the stones beneath the double gate and realized I stood in one of the few places where we can say with absolute certainty, "Jesus walked here." If Jesus exited the Temple that day from this gate—and He probably did—then His last steps ever on the Temple Mount were taken on the ground where I stood.

I walked to the southwest corner of the Temple Mount and looked north along its Western Wall. What I saw there represented Jesus' words to His disciples fulfilled.

Sponsored by a distinguished member of the Jewish Federation of Metropolitan Detroit (the owner of the Detroit Pistons), an excavation has uncovered a first-century street dating to before the Temple's destruction in A.D. 70. The 30-foot-wide street had pavement made of stone slabs, some up to a foot thick. The pavement had been literally crushed and pressed into the ground by the massive stones hurled down from above. Excavators uncovered most of the street but left one pile of stones just as they found them to show what had happened.

I remembered Jesus' words: "Not one stone will be left upon another which will not be torn down." The Romans hurled the stones from the Temple down into this street, crushing the pavement.

One stone on the ground at the southwest corner had a Hebrew inscription on it: "To the place of trumpeting." I squinted up to the top of the wall from near where this stone would have fallen. Priests would have stood there overlooking the city to blow the shofar, which announced the Sabbath and the start of festival days. Some say this represented the pinnacle of the Temple. If so, Jesus would have stood beside this stone when Satan tempted Him to jump down, forcing God to save Him and impressing the crowds that He was the Christ— all a temptation to grab the glory without the cross (see chapter 2).

127

Just north of the street on which I stood, the Western Wall plaza had dozens of Jews rocking and praying before the wall. They face the wall because it remains the closest they can get to the place where the Temple stood. Ironically, they stand atop 30 feet of rubble consisting of stones from the destroyed Temple they lament.

Before I left, I stopped before a place in the wall where someone had long ago scratched a verse in Hebrew. Just below a tuft of bush read a paraphrase of Isaiah 66:14: "And you shall see and your heart shall rejoice and their bones like grass shall . . ."—the rest was gone. Later I looked up the whole verse. It speaks of a time when the kingdom of the Messiah will dispense mercy to His servants and anger to His enemies.

Isn't it a bit presumptuous—and precarious—to pray for the justice of the Kingdom without first becoming a servant of the King?

I still have the T-shirt my grandmother bought me when she went to Jerusalem in 1987. (Some of us keep clothes *way* too long.) Printed in English, Hebrew and Arabic, the shirt celebrated "The 20th Anniversary of the Reunification of Jerusalem." Now more than 20 years later still—and more than 60 years since the beginning of the State of Israel—the land has just as much tension and heartache as ever. And much of the conflict cloaks its true motives in the name of religion.

Outside the Jaffa Gate, I saw a banner draped across a bridge. The sign included a creative blend of images and letters, which formed a word. An Islamic crescent moon represented the first letter, C. Then after the letters o and e came the Star of David, which symbolized the letter X. After two more letters, i and s, the word ended with a Christian cross, signifying the letter T. Putting it all together, it read "CoeXisT." I shook my head when I saw it.

The banner's suggestion that Islam, Judaism and Christianity can coexist in the Holy Land—or anywhere, for that matter—makes great fodder for political speeches. But it only ends up working itself out in wars and rumors of wars. Peace among contradicting worldviews always sounds like a good idea until someone breaks into your home and threatens your family. At that point, the course of action is plain—peace comes from violent protection.

During Israel's 1947-48 struggle for independence, only one place in Jerusalem enjoyed the peaceful coexistence of Jews and Arabs—the government insane asylum. A delegate of the International Red Cross, Jacques de Reynier, saw the patients' lack of concern for the conflict in Jerusalem. He scribbled in his diary three words: *"Vive les fous!"*—"Long live the nuts!"[3]

The syncretism of modern Judaism began long before the last century. I remember seeing a large mosaic in the central hall of the Hammat Tiberias Synagogue, built in the third century A.D. The mosaic portrayed Jewish symbols, like a seven-branch menorah, a box to hold the Torah, an incense shovel and shofars. But right next to these lay the signs of the zodiac—all in Hebrew! This synagogue represented the same time period when the Talmud and Mishnah were developed. Some suggest the mosaic represented Judaism's triumph over paganism. That sounds great, but it's no excuse for the images there. More likely, the mosaic reveals the syncretism already in bloom in Jesus' day—a foreshadowing of modern, liberal Judaism.

Without taking away any of the dignity of their tradition, I personally found it difficult to connect with the Jews' rocking before the Wall.

But wait.

What about *my* traditions? Are they any less bizarre to others, any less potentially hypocritical—even though I know the true Lord and Savior?

Jews pray with their heads covered; we take our hats off. Their prayers are public and loud and showy; ours are private and quiet and restrained. They rock back and forth and mumble from a book; we bow our heads, close our eyes and utter unrehearsed words.

But even our "extemporaneous" prayers follow traditions, don't they? Ever heard those who mutter "Father God" in almost every sentence they pray? What about bowing our heads and closing our eyes— where is *that* in the Bible? Even praying "in Jesus' name" has become little more than a verbal cue for the end of a prayer. In fact, I dare you to end a public prayer without it and see if it doesn't at least *feel* odd— almost like sacrilege. Someone may even question you on it.

129

It's easy in the familiarity of our own traditions to shake our fingers at the oddities of others. Jews pray while rocking, Muslims kneel with their bottoms in the air, and we bow our heads and close our eyes. But without the heart engaged, our worship becomes as hypocritical as those who don't know the true God. Blend any tradition— bowing, standing, prostrating, rocking, kneeling or jumping—with no personal relationship with God, and it's totally pointless.

Before meals, my grandfather used to pray the same short prayer in Spanish. And while I didn't understand a word of it, I could soon repeat it verbatim. My bedtime prayers as a boy followed the same pattern: "Now I lay me down to sleep, I pray the Lord my soul to keep...." I could rattle that puppy off in about 10 seconds. But my heart was not in it.

Even these days, old habits die hard. After giving thanks for dinner one evening, I opened my eyes to see one of my daughters just staring at me. "Do you know you pray the same thing every time?" she asked. *From the mouths of babes.* So the next night I made sure to pray from the heart. "You changed it!" she exclaimed.

The unbelief Jesus taught against was not an unbelief in the existence of God but one in which people lived *as though* He did not exist. The Pharisees did their good deeds for others to notice.

Frankly, I often do as well. Maybe you do, too.

I remember seeing at both Masada and Beersheba a one-inch painted black line running across the walls of the ruins. This line revealed the division between the original ruins below and the modern reconstruction built directly on top of it. In some places, if not for the line, I could make no distinction between the real and the reconstruction.

Unfortunately, we have no black line running down our lives and behaviors to reveal the division between the authentic and the phony. The line often seems easy to see in the lives of others, but discerning it in ourselves—that proves a challenge, even when we're looking for it.

When a federal court order removed the Ten Commandments monument from the rotunda of the Judicial Building in Montgomery, Alabama, Christians went nuts with protests. But as believers, we have to be careful about becoming more concerned about the removal of a monument of Scripture than we are about living what the stone represents. The presence of a monument no more indicates the godliness of a nation than do the Bibles in our laps.

Do we live what we say we believe? Where we don't, we must face our hypocrisy. God cares far less about our monuments in stone than He cares about His Word in our hearts (see Jer. 31:33). And He doesn't mind removing or destroying the monuments—or Temples—to prove His point.

God never intended for us to display His Word as a museum prop without also displaying His Word in our lives. From the gold-leafed Guttenberg Bible in the Library of Congress in Washington, DC, to the great Isaiah scroll encased in the Shrine of the Book in Jerusalem—our biblical monuments and mementos should reflect biblical motives. Otherwise, they simply mock our hypocrisy.

We always have to come back to the simple truth that Jesus refused to commend *any* religious activity that was not an expression of character. If our good and spiritual behavior fails to express our hearts, then our behavior is hypocrisy. This is why the Bible remains so adamant about the renewal of the mind (see Ps. 119:9-11, Prov. 23:7; Rom. 12:1-3; Col. 3:1-10). Because only with a renewed mind comes a new life.

—m—

I grabbed a slice of pizza from my favorite café and descended some stairs to explore the ancient, excavated Cardo Street. "Cardo" means "heart," and this main thoroughfare of Byzantine Jerusalem ran through the heart of the city, north to the Damascus Gate.

I passed an enlarged reproduction of a portion of the Medeba map that showed "The Holy City of Jerusalem," written in Greek. The original sixth-century mosaic rests in a church floor in Medeba, Jordan, and illustrates the many columns that once lined Cardo Street. I could see some of them as I walked.

Behind a tall glass case stood a six-foot menorah on a raised platform—the first golden menorah constructed since the destruction of the Temple. This massive candle stand represents just one of many articles the Temple Institute has prepared for the future Jewish Temple—whenever it rises. They have everything ready. All they need now is a Messiah.

Just then, in the street above me, I heard the distinctive sound of live music from a single violin. Wanting to get some video of authentic music, I choked down my pizza and bounded up the stairs two at a time. Following my ears, I found the musician, a woman about 60 years old.

She wore a thin navy blouse with white flowers. Her short hair framed a round, rugged face and deep blue eyes. She stood alone and unnoticed as people passed. When she saw me approach and stop, her wrinkled face pinched a smile.

"Will you play something Jewish?" I asked, dropping some shekels into her open case.

She nodded and began a soulful rendition of "Yerushalaim Shel Zahav" ("Jerusalem of Gold"). Her instrument looked dull and worn and in need of cleaning. Her long vibratos seemed exaggerated, and I marveled at how her pudgy hand could play a fingerboard so small.

The melody she shaped has lyrics that translate into Israel's hope, much like the nearby golden menorah that waits for a rebuilt Temple:

> *A shofar calls out on the Temple Mount in the Old City.*
> *And in the caves in the mountain, thousands of suns shine.*
> *We will once again descend to the Dead Sea by way of Jericho!*
> *Jerusalem of gold, and of bronze and of light,*
> *Behold, I am a violin for all your songs.*

I thought back to a night at the Western Wall when I observed a military ceremony that inducted new soldiers into the Israeli Defense Force. Propane torches atop military tripods lit the plaza, while alternating blue and white plastic flags roped off the area. I got as close as I could.

A single trumpet fanfare began the formal ceremony and evoked the same mood in me as when I hear "Taps." At least a hundred soldiers, both men and women, stood at attention. Their crisp tan uniforms, black berets and rifles seemed misplaced on those so young.

The loudspeaker began Israel's national anthem, "Hatikvah" ("The Hope") and the saluting soldiers sang as one with passion and pride. It seemed as if they truly knew their efforts would help fulfill the words they sang in Hebrew:

> *As long as the Jewish spirit is yearning deep in the heart,*
> *With eyes turned toward the East, looking toward Zion,*
> *Then our hope—the two-thousand-year-old hope—will not be lost:*
> *To be a free people in our land,*
> *The land of Zion and Jerusalem.*

The loudspeaker uttered short Hebrew phrases with "Israel" in them, which the soldiers repeated loudly in unison. A prayer followed, in which I recognized the Lord's name, "Adonai." But during the prayer, the ultra-orthodox Jews at the Wall—the religious community of the nation—continued rocking as if nothing was happening behind them. The disconnect disturbed me.

Soft symphonic renditions of "Hatikvah" continued in the background while each soldier's name rang out across the plaza and echoed off the Wall. The crowd erupted in applause. I couldn't help but feel drawn to their national pride.

"Very good," I told the violinist when she finished her song. "Can you play something else, something Jewish?"

She paused. "Something classical? I'm trained classical."

I shook my head and smiled, "Something Jewish."

"Jewish," she repeated. She searched the trees for inspiration, a bit embarrassed. Then her eyes brightened, and she raised her bow to the instrument. I immediately recognized the familiar air of "Hava Nagila" ("Let Us Rejoice"). She performed the opening verse with short, rhythmic jerks. The loose horsehairs of her bow danced to the tune whose repetitive lyrics offer a simple invitation:

133

> Let's rejoice and be happy!
> Let's sing and be happy!
> Awake, brothers, with a happy heart!

I recently saw a televised concert commemorating the Israel Philharmonic Orchestra's seventieth anniversary. Originally named the Palestine Philharmonic Orchestra in 1937, the ensemble changed their name when Israel became a nation. On May 14, 1948, David Ben Gurion spoke on behalf of the Jewish people and declared Israel's independence as a state in accordance with the United Nations' new resolution. The renamed Israel Philharmonic performed "Hatikvah," the new nation's anthem. (When I visited Ben Gurion's modest home in the Negev, I noticed in his vast library a surprising volume: *Things to Come*, by J. Dwight Pentecost—a hardback explaining the Bible's fulfillment of Israel's hope through the Messiah, Jesus Christ.)

The day following Israel's declaration, the surrounding Arab nations mounted an all-out attack on Israel, eventually blockading the Jews within Jerusalem in a modern siege. The late violinist Isaac Stern recounted that when the first supply truck finally broke through the lines to bring critical support to Jerusalem, the Jews made a request of the truck for its next trip: "Please bring music." Stern added that music became as essential to the Jews as bread.

Following the Six-Day War in 1967, the Israel Philharmonic performed a concert on the scorching slopes of Mount Scopus, overlooking the newly reunified Jerusalem. No longer prohibited from the Old City, the Jews controlled all of Jerusalem for the first time since the Bar Kokhba Revolt in A.D. 132. However, the conflict over the land remains to this day.

Isaac Stern—who became the celebrated soloist in the Oscar-winning soundtrack *Fiddler on the Roof*—told of his first visit to the Western Wall after the Mount Scopus concert. He and other members of the orchestra put their prayers on slips of paper and in the wall. "I put my prayer in the Wall as others did . . . and should," Stern remembered. "But my prayer has not yet been answered. I prayed for peace."

"One more, please," I requested when the violinist cadenced. "Something else Jewish." If I had requested Mendelssohn, her face would have wrinkled with delight. Instead, her brow furrowed as she consented.

After a moment, her violin began the slow, mournful strains of "Ose Shalom" ("The One Who Makes Peace"). Her tone squeaked and her pitch faltered a few beats flat, betraying the infrequency with which she performed such requests. But the melody's imperfection seemed appropriate, like a frail voice mourning the words of a song too wonderful to be true:

> *May the One who makes peace, make peace above—*
> *Make peace over us and over all Israel.*
> *And let us say, Amen.*

As she repeated the song an octave higher, the sounds of Israel's hope rose from that Jerusalem street like a prayer—more like a plea—ascending to God.

All Israel needs is a Messiah to make *hatikvah*—the hope—a reality.

But first He had to die.

Notes

1. Paul J. Achtemeier, *Harper's Bible Dictionary*, 1st ed. (San Francisco: Harper and Row, and Society of Biblical Literature, 1985), p. 463.
2. Harold W. Hoehner, *Chronological Aspects of the Life of Christ* (Grand Rapids, MI: Zondervan Publishing House, 1977); see also Alva J. McClain, *Daniel's Prophecy of the Seventy Weeks* (Grand Rapids: Zondervan Publishing House, 1969).
3. Larry Collins and Dominique LaPierre, *O Jerusalem!* (Israel: Steimatzky House, 1993), pp. 123-124.

CHAPTER SEVEN

UPSTAIRS WITH JESUS

"Father, forgive them; for they do not know what they are doing."
LUKE 23:34

"Go and prepare the Passover for us, so that we may eat it" (Luke 22:8).

"Where do You want us to prepare it?" Peter and John asked Jesus (v. 9).

"When you have entered the city, a man will meet you carrying a pitcher of water; follow him into the house that he enters" (v. 10). "The owner of the house," Jesus continued, "will show you a large, furnished upper room; prepare it there" (vv. 11-12).

In the southern part of Jerusalem stands the Cenacle—from the Latin word *cena*, for "dinner"—the traditional location of the Last Supper. To get to the Upper Room, the disciples had to enter the city of Jerusalem. But to get there today, one has to leave the Old City walls. I headed in that direction.

A scent and a sound caught my attention. A local Jew with a pushcart full of freshly baked bread hollered to me. I knew what he asked without understanding his words. I bought part of a loaf from him and ate it as I walked.

I left the Old City walls through the Zion Gate, so named for its access to modern Mount Zion on the Western Hill. After I exited, a compact car immediately followed, its wheels squeaking on the polished stones as it slowly navigated the tight left turn within the gate. I paused on the other side of the street to examine the Zion Gate, still pockmarked with bullet holes from the struggle to liberate the Jewish Quarter in the 1948 War of Independence.

Arabs call the gate *Bab Nabi Daud*, "Gate of the Prophet David," because King David's tomb allegedly rests on "Mount Zion." Byzantine Christians in the fifth century confused the Western Hill with Mount Zion and so gave rise to some regrettable misnomers. In addition to misnaming the hill, they mistook Herod's palace for David's, and today the "Tower of David" stands as part of the Citadel.

The actual biblical Mount Zion sits east of where I stood, across the Central Valley, and included the ancient City of David and the Temple Mount. David rests somewhere over there (see 1 Kings 2:10; Neh. 3:16; Acts 2:29).

I made my way south, past the sprawling, beautiful hundred-year-old Dormition Abbey, with its huge cone-shaped dome and white stones. Not much further along, I saw a plain sign with one word painted in Hebrew: "David." The arrow pointed into a small courtyard.

I entered a cramped room barely large enough for its only piece of "furniture." Several Jews prayed before what looked like a casket. It gave me the feeling of a wake or attending a visitation, and the room's mood matched it. Behind a black handrail with a padlocked gate, a cenotaph (tomb marker or monument) lay draped in dark purple velvet with the Star of David embroidered on it in gold thread. This marker was supposedly built over the tomb of David, but this monument was placed on the wrong hill.

Before the reunification of Jerusalem in 1967, Jews could not enter the Old City to worship at the Western Wall as they can today. So, many Jews prayed here instead . . . and some still do. On top of the cenotaph, I saw silver crowns and arks of Torah scrolls from synagogues throughout the world—Jewish relics rescued from the Nazi Holocaust.

I found it ironic that the hope of all Israel—the hope that every Jew prays for when he or she bows here before David's memory—was spoken of by the Son of David Himself in the room just above.

Since the first century, believers have venerated this site as the location where Jesus ate the Last Supper with His disciples. I walked up about 30 steps and followed our group around to a large upper room. Lit like a cavern with dramatic lighting, the bright space had slabs of stone for flooring and a tall ceiling supported by gothic arches. Crusaders rebuilt the second-story room much as it appears today, though during an intervening time, Muslims installed a prayer niche and Arabic inscriptions in stained-glass windows to claim the place as their own.

Of course, the room looked nothing like this when Jesus and His men reclined to eat the Passover. But knowing that this room occupied the same air space as the original room allowed me still to imagine the words Jesus spoke here that night.

"I have earnestly desired to eat this Passover with you before I suffer," Jesus told the Twelve as they began, "for I say to you, I shall never again eat it until it is fulfilled in the kingdom of God" (Luke 22:15-16). *Ah yes, the kingdom of God.* The disciples never forgot Jesus' promise that when He sits on His glorious throne, they too will sit on thrones and judge the tribes of Israel. As they reclined at the table, Jesus reiterated that promise (see Matt. 19:28; Luke 22:29-30).

When these men had entered the home, no house servant had performed the usual menial task of washing their dirty feet. I bet Jesus arranged it that way.

Walking on concrete at most tourist stops kept my shoes and sandals relatively clean in Jerusalem. But after a day of hiking in Petra, Jordan, with each step lifting clouds of dust, my feet turned *completely* gray up to mid-calf. What a mess! Mixed with the sweat from the heat of the day, the dirt muddied the hairs on my calves. What do you think I did before dinner that night? Washed those feet!

So why didn't one of the disciples volunteer to scrub the feet of the group? Because, remember, these guys were celebrities—famous all over Israel. In fact, they even began *to argue* amongst themselves about which of them was considered the greatest (see Luke 22:24). The disciples' pride swelled and left no space in the room for a menial footwasher. Imagine these "great" men reclining to eat the Passover with the Son of God—but with 12 sets of filthy feet!

When Jesus arose, stripped and condescended to clean the feet of the Twelve—including Judas's—Peter protested with words that revealed the arrogance of the whole lot: "Never shall You wash my feet!" (John 13:8). How pious. It wasn't an objection because of Jesus' greatness as much as because of Peter's pride. Notice, Peter waited until Jesus came to *him* before he objected.

A mere week earlier, as they had walked up the Ascent of Adummim from Jericho, Jesus had taught them that greatness and servanthood *go together* in God's kingdom (see Mark 10:45). But they didn't remember. Even Jesus' week of preaching against the hypocrisy of the religious leaders had bounced off the disciples' pride like pebbles off a stone wall. It would take more than words to crumble their hard hearts.

So while they were eating, Jesus dropped another bomb.

"Truly I say to you that one of you will betray Me" (Matt. 26:21).

I would love to have seen that moment. If there had been a piano player in the room, he would have stopped in utter silence. Picture it: The disciples just stared at one another. And then, one by one, they each revealed their blind pride by opening their mouths: "Surely, not I, Lord?" (Matt. 26:22; see also Mark 14:19; John 13:22). They were at a loss to guess who Jesus meant, never considering any one of themselves as a candidate. Even Judas chimed in, "Surely it is not I, Rabbi?"— even though he had already secured the deal to betray Jesus to the chief priests (Matt. 26:25; see also Matt. 26:14-16,25; Mark 14:10-11; Luke 22:3-6).

139

After Jesus sent Judas out with Satan in tow (or vice versa), the Lord told the Eleven that they would all fall away that very night. "But after I have been raised," Jesus added mercifully, "I will go ahead of you to Galilee" (Mark 14:28). A significant promise—ignored.

"Even though all may fall away, yet I will not!" Peter blurted (Mark 14:29; see also Luke 22:33). Wow . . . I bet the other 10 applauded that remark. *These others may blow it, Lord, but I never will!* Can you imagine?

Jesus' gentle words to the immature man gave a perspective very, very few of us ever remember in trials: "Simon, Simon, behold, Satan has demanded permission to sift you like wheat; but I have prayed for you, that your faith may not fail; and you, when once you have turned again, strengthen your brothers" (Luke 22:31-32). These two verses burst with theology and give dawn to our dark understanding of spiritual warfare. Read them again. Every word Jesus spoke to Peter remains true of us in temptation—including the obligation that follows restoration.

Jesus not only predicted Peter's denial but also Peter's repentance! Yet the big fisherman—who really *needed* to hear words of hope—ignored Jesus' good news and reacted only to the bad. Christ quickly gave Peter the bitter pill, telling him that before a rooster crowed that very night, he would deny Him three times (see Mark 14:30). Peter, of course, denied that he would deny.

"Even if I have to die with You, I will not deny You!" Peter crowed (Matt. 26:35; Mark 14:31). Don't you wish just saying something made it true?

—⁂—

Most of us Christians have experienced those incredible moments of intimacy with God when we have no yearning for any earthly joy, much less for sin. Christ becomes our *entire* desire. In times like those, we want to build a few tabernacles and just bask in the Transfiguration. In those moments, we make impassioned commitments of absolute dedication. We really believe we have turned a corner in our spiritual lives.

But then, driving away from church, our family disagrees over where to eat. Or after our quiet time, our bickering children rapidly rob us of joy. Or on the way to work, a hurried driver cuts us off and waves with only a fraction of his hand. All of a sudden, commitment wanes. And these are the little things. What about real life crises?

Jesus knows our weaknesses. He understands that the crosses we bear can often obscure our destination. And Jesus knew that night that the braggarts with Him in the Upper Room would all fall away.

So He instituted for them—and for us—a memorial that would repeatedly bring us back to the greatest source of motivation in the Christian life. "This is My body which is given for you; do this in remembrance of Me," Jesus told them. "This cup which is poured out for you is the new covenant in My blood" (Luke 22:19-20).

Eating bread and drinking the fruit of the vine represent a recognition that His body was "given for you," and His blood was "poured out for you." The "Last Supper" has become the Lord's Supper—a memorial of Jesus and His amazing love, which He displayed in His death.

Christ gave His disciples two ordinances, but both have prerequisites. Baptism occurs once and requires a person to be a believer in Jesus. The Lord's Supper occurs repeatedly and requires a believer to examine him- or herself prior to participation each time (see 1 Cor. 11:27). Baptism represents forgiveness and conversion to Christ; the Lord's Supper represents fellowship and communion with Christ.

The Lord's Supper points us *backward* to Jesus' death for our sins, *inward* at our present walk with Jesus and *forward* to Jesus' coming again. "For as often as you eat this bread and drink the cup," the apostle Paul would later write, "you proclaim the Lord's death until He comes" (1 Cor. 11:26).

So what's our motivation when life challenges our devotion? "He died for all, so that they who live might no longer live for themselves, but for Him who died and rose again on their behalf" (2 Cor. 5:15). He had no obligation to forgive our sins, only to judge them. Our response comes as one of gratitude. We respond in light of God's grace and mercy.

141

On one trip to Israel, I went without my family for over three weeks—the longest time I've ever spent away from them. And while I spoke with them regularly the whole time I traveled, the last conversation is the one I'll never forget. After weeks of separation, we all felt eager to see one another again. I can still hear my younger daughter's words from the other side of the world: "It's like I don't even know you, Daddy." *Open heart, insert battle-axe.* A mere three weeks apart made our relationship seem surreal. I've thought about her comment often as I considered Christ's words to His headstrong disciples that night. The same principle applies.

"Apart from Me you can do nothing" (John 15:5). *Nothing.* That word seems so conclusive, so dreadfully final. Our success hinges on our remaining in fellowship with Jesus.

I remember a day at Neot Kedumim, the biblical landscape preserve in Israel, where our group strolled among many plants spoken of in the Bible. Our guide at the preserve, a passionate Jewish lady named Helen, picked a small hyssop branch and led us to a tall cedar of Lebanon, donated by the Lebanese army. We hushed to listen.

"The cedar of Lebanon is always an import," she began. "It will grow to a height of well over 120 feet. It is a symbol of haughtiness, pride and glamour." We huddled in closer so we could hear over the noise of the military training in the distance. "We remember the story of David and Bathsheba, and we have the hint in Psalm 51 of David's real sin, when he asks: 'Cleanse me with hyssop that I may be pure'" (see Ps. 51:7).

She held up the hyssop branch with its white blossoms. Rarely did flowers bloom in May, she told us.

"David in his prayer is asking for forgiveness not for the sin of adultery, not for the sin of murder, but for the sin of pride. 'Cleanse me with hyssop—humility—so that I'll remember who I really am. I am your servant and not a great big fancy king.'" She even mentioned how hyssop was used when Jesus died on the cross, explaining, "He is the symbol of humility among men."

142

I thought about her metaphor and how Scripture takes the hyssop allusions much further than as a symbol of humility. The hyssop's blooms served as an excellent sponge and found their use in a number of sacrificial rites in Israel—beginning with applying the blood of the Passover lamb to the doorway during the Exodus (see Exod. 12:22; cf. Lev. 14:4ff; Num. 19:18). In fact, out of the 12 uses of "hyssop" in the Bible, 11 occur in the context of purification.

David's prayer uses hyssop as a metaphor that indicates the means of his forgiveness: through the blood of a sacrifice. The New Testament adds, "Without shedding of blood there is no forgiveness" (Heb. 9:22). I find it fascinating that the only mention of hyssop in the Gospels comes at the very moment Jesus completed His work of redemption, fulfilling His sacrificial atonement as the final Passover Lamb (see John 19:29-30).

Nothing. That word has such a haunting finality, doesn't it? If we fail to remain in fellowship with Jesus, we can do nothing—not "some things," not "a few things"—but *no thing*. Nothing of any lasting spiritual value whatsoever. But *with* Jesus, on the other hand, nothing is impossible that is His will (see Matt. 19:26).

Because a believers' salvation remains secure, the Lord's Supper is an opportunity to evaluate and celebrate fellowship with Jesus. Christ commanded the memorial *to keep us* in fellowship with Him so that we may bear much fruit for God's glory (see John 15:1-16).

The disciples received a message of hope that night as they reclined upstairs with Jesus. He promised that though He would leave shortly, He would send the Holy Spirit to dwell with them. And one day Jesus would return to take them to heaven (see John 13:33–14:17).

After leaving the Upper Room that day, I paused again at the "Tomb of David." I reflected on how the blood of the New Covenant—Jesus' blood, which He spoke of upstairs—provided the final means for answering David's prayer for forgiveness. Christ's mercy in shedding His blood and the hope that His resurrection offers are the motivation by which we live a life of obedience to His Word (see Rom. 12:1; 1 Pet. 1:3). His sacrifice even provided the means by which He will one day satisfy "the hope" of every Jewish prayer.

143

—※—

Jesus and the Eleven sang a hymn as they departed the Upper Room. But like the Psalms of Ascents they chanted the week before on the trip up to Jerusalem, the words took a nosedive from the disciples' lips that night.

The dozen crossed the Kidron Valley and, as the Mount of Olives began to rise, entered into an olive grove at a place called Gethsemane (see Mark 14:32; John 18:1).

For the triumphal entry five days earlier, Jesus' descent from the crest could have occurred in only one area. The topography of the land in antiquity lent itself to one route of descent, roughly the modern road that descends from Et Tur. Another modern road runs closely parallel to it from the ridge, the steep descent I walked to the Dominus Flevit Church, where Jesus wept. These two paths converge at the bottom of the hill near the Garden of Gethsemane, where He would weep again on this night after the Passover meal.

Gethsemane means "oil press," the remains of which were dis-covered in a small cave at the base of the hill. As I entered the grotto, a stone bowl affixed to the wall offered holy water. The small cave—a room really—held two dozen folding chairs facing an altar and a cru-cifix. A priest paced the floor with a feather brush, dusting the small stone altar. On the cave wall behind him, I saw a painting of Jesus in a red robe, hands and eyes raised, His face beaming. The disciples semicircled behind Him, some folding their hands in prayer and oth-ers covering their faces. The painting depicted them in the cave where I stood. Most interesting to me though—and most accurate—were the bronze statuettes of two disciples, sitting and leaning against the base of the altar—asleep!

Byzantine Christians believed that this cave marked the place where Jesus left eight of His men, taking Peter, James and John with Him into the nearby garden to pray.

"My soul is deeply grieved, to the point of death," Jesus told the three; "remain here and keep watch with Me" (Matt. 26:38; see also Mark 14:34). Jesus also told them, "Pray that you may not enter into temptation"—a principle He had taught them before in the "Lord's Prayer." But that probably seemed so long ago (Luke 22:40; cf. 8:13; 11:4).

The section of the Garden of Gethsemane that tourists get to visit lies behind the walled courtyard of the Church of All Nations. The small garden, about 50 feet square, sits behind a handrail that encloses and protects it. Only about a dozen ancient trees grow in the garden. The massive, gnarled trunks produce new shoots, their leaves gray and thin. Gravel pathways section off the manicured garden, with white, yellow, blue, red and orange blooms accenting the trees. When I was there, even butterflies flitted about the picture-perfect scene. Chirping sparrows reminded me of Jesus' statement that He values me much more than them (see Matt. 10:31). I wish there had been benches to sit on.

Suddenly, I heard the screeching of tires and that awful, blunt crunch from cars colliding. I impulsively looked toward the street, but the wall kept my curiosity inside the garden.

"Bummer," someone noted.

What an odd place to hear a collision, I thought. I looked again at the garden but now listened beyond the wall. I saw peace and tranquility, but I heard cars honking, brakes squealing, belts slipping and gears shifting. Peaceful serenity mixed with turmoil, neither affecting the other.

In a strange way, the scene struck me as similar to what Jesus might have experienced the night He fell to the ground and cried out to the Father. The Church of All Nations covers the traditional spot where Jesus prayed in agony—yet at the same time, He prayed with perfect confidence in the Father. Peace amidst turmoil.

At the front of the church, four groupings of columns support a massive mosaic, which crowns the facade. It depicts Christ gazing up in prayer to the Father who holds the alpha and omega letters. Angels hover near Jesus, and the disciples bow to His left and right.

I entered the church and my eyes were drawn upward. Large arches lift a ceiling decorated like a night sky with stars shining and olive branches reaching upward—much like Jesus would have seen the night He prayed here. Various mosaics and paintings on the walls—all elaborate and beautiful—depict scenes from that agonizing night. Candles, benches and altars accommodate the various traditions of worshippers who mill about. Surprisingly, it was silent.

145

A large altar against the center of the back wall overshadows a bare outcropping of rock on the floor. I walked up as close as I could to this spot where it is believed Jesus bowed in prayer. Person after person approached, knelt and kissed the rock blackened by decades of lips pressed in the same spot.

Again, I found it difficult not to presume insincerity in the hearts of the worshippers simply because I don't share their tradition. "Kiss the Son," David had written, not "Kiss the stone" (Ps. 2:12, *NIV*). When I see Jews kissing a mezuzah (a case with a scroll of Scripture inside of it) on their doorposts, I think of them as devoted. But when I see Christians kissing rocks, it bothers me. I guess the inconsistency of my reasoning reveals my own hypocrisy. For all I know, they love the Lord Jesus far more than I do.

The 10-square-foot mass of limestone, called the Rock of Agony, has a wrought-iron vine of thorns surrounding it on three sides, each side depicting two birds with a cup between them. I had no idea what the birds represent, but the cup obviously points to Jesus' prayer that night. My imagination entered the scene.

"Father, if You are willing, remove this cup from Me; yet not My will, but Yours be done" (Luke 22:42; see also Matt. 26:39; Mark 14:36).

Luke's Gospel relates that Jesus prayed so fervently, in such agony, that His sweat fell as thick as drops of blood (see Luke 22:44). Most people believe Jesus prayed this prayer because He dreaded the physical torture ahead. I think He also pled with the Father because Jesus knew what His crucifixion would produce: *separation* from the Father—*spiritual death*.

In all eternity past, Jesus had never experienced the separation that faced Him the next day.

146

—⚏—

Every one of us has prayed the first half of Jesus' prayer. But the second half? That checkout line has a shorter number of people.

I have discovered that the most difficult battles in life simply mirror Christ's struggle in Gethsemane. By far my greatest challenges come not from those circumstances that press in upon me, but from the internal struggle to surrender my will to God. I enter Gethsemane daily and have to drag my will to the Father in prayer. So do you.

When someone for whom we've prayed for years dies unrepentant—"*Not my will, but Yours be done.*" When living as a godly spouse, parent or single proves enormously harder than we ever imagined—"*Not my will, but Yours be done.*" When we lose a job and suddenly face an uncertain future—"*Not my will, but Yours be done.*" When a child is born with a physical or mental defect—"*Not my will, but Yours be done.*" The list only ends when life does.

Life will hand you what seems like a raw deal. And when God's will seems cruel to you and not good, you will wage no greater battle than the surrender of your will. At that moment, when God's goodness seems a hypocritical pile of hogwash, you stand only inches away from using anger to justify your sin.

But I promise you, surrender lies at the very core of whatever grieves you today. And surrendering in absolute trust to the Father—as Jesus did in Gethsemane—remains the only path to peace. Especially when you can make no sense of it all.

I noticed a Latin phrase carved into the façade of the Church of All Nations, just below the mosaic of Jesus praying. No verse reference was included to clue me in on the translation, so I later showed my daughters' Latin teacher a picture of the façade. As she slowly began to translate, I recognized the verse from Hebrews 5:7: "He offered up prayers and petitions with loud cries and tears, . . . and he was heard because of his reverent submission" (*NIV*). Somebody knew their stuff to put that verse there.

Did Jesus prefer not to suffer physical and spiritual torment? Well, of course. But Jesus had a greater desire: to do the Father's will—*whatever that meant.*

When Jesus rose from prayer, soaked in sweat, He came to the disciples and found that they had fallen asleep.

"Why are you sleeping? Get up and pray that you may not enter into temptation" (Luke 22:46).

If you do a word study on "temptation" in the Gospels, you see it occurring like bookends in Jesus' ministry. Temptation arose first in the wilderness after His baptism and finally at Gethsemane before His death (see Luke 4:13; 22:40,46). In both instances, Jesus resisted the temptation to satisfy His own desires and instead clung to God's Word and God's will.

Three times Jesus prayed, and three times He found the disciples sleeping. These same men—who demanded only hours earlier that they would die with Jesus before falling away—were not even willing to pray with Him. It's always easier to die for Jesus than to live for Him.

The words Jesus had spoken to the religious leaders also proved true of His disciples. And lest we feel too pious, they often also bespeak our own hypocrisy: "Rightly did Isaiah prophesy of you hypocrites, as it is written, 'This people honors Me with their lips, but their heart is far away from Me'" (Matt. 15:8).

Lips were used for more than insincere words that night.

The sounds of a mob's hushed voices and footsteps grew louder as they approached the garden. The clanking of swords, clubs, torches and lanterns fell silent as the mass stood still at a distance. Judas approached alone.

"Greetings, Rabbi!" the betrayer gushed, and he kissed Jesus—signaling whom the lynch mob should arrest.

Jesus' final words to Judas would ring in his ears throughout eternity: "Judas, are you betraying the Son of Man with a kiss?" (Luke 22:48).

The *shing* of Peter's sword being jerked from its scabbard was followed by the screams of the now-one-eared servant of the high priest. Jesus reached out and healed him. "Put the sword into the sheath," Jesus commanded Peter; "the cup which the Father has given Me, shall I not drink it?" (John 18:11).

148

"The cup"—that should have rung a bell with the disciples. Earlier that night Jesus had passed a cup to His men—the cup that represented His suffering—and they all willingly drank from it. But now, as the cup's metaphor became reality, only Jesus would take a sip.

The Lord's predictions of Judas's betrayal and the disciples' desertion found their fulfillment in the same scene. In the terror of self-preservation, Jesus' closest friends tore off in 11 directions like rabbits, leaving Him all alone—arrested and bound. On the same hill where the disciples had hailed Him as Messiah five days earlier, they all deserted Him to save their own skin.

"Are you able to drink the cup that I drink, or to be baptized with the baptism with which I am baptized?" (Mark 10:38). Jesus had asked James and John this question only the previous week (see chapter 5). As the "Sons of Thunder" zigzagged through the olive trees on their sprint out of the dark garden, I wonder if their answer to Jesus' question now chased them as an accusation.

"We are able," they had blathered.

Their pace never slowed.

—⟨⟩—

The soldiers and Jewish officials dragged Jesus back across the Kidron Valley, through the ancient City of David, into the Central Valley and up the Western Hill—probably retracing the path Jesus took only hours earlier with His disciples. I crossed the Kidron once at night—totally a different experience than during the day.

Six trials total—three religious and three civil—all occurred in a mockery of justice. Jesus first stood before Annas, the father-in-law of Caiaphas, the high priest. Then Caiaphas himself questioned Jesus in the high priest's house at night, with no credible witnesses and not in the Temple—all the makings of an unlawful hearing.

I walked up an ancient street that ascends from the valley floor to one of the traditional locations for the house of Caiaphas. Some suggest the mob dragged Jesus up this same stone staircase to Caiaphas's home. Built over the ruins of the home today is a church bearing the name Church of St. Peter in Gallicantu.

Peter and another unnamed disciple, perhaps John, sprinted only far enough to circle and observe from a distance. They followed Jesus up into the courtyard of the high priest's home, and Peter began to warm himself beside a charcoal fire with the soldiers (see John 18:18). As Peter sat in the firelight, a servant girl eyed him closely and identified him as a disciple of Jesus. Her charge reduced Peter to a liar.

"I do not know what you are talking about," Peter hedged (Matt. 26:70).

I noticed the church has large bronze doors with a relief depicting Jesus holding up three fingers and pointing at Peter. The disciple's gesture, in contrast, boasts self-confidence, with a rooster perched in the window. Above the church's doorway is a Latin verse etched on the lintel: "The LORD will guard your going out and your coming in" (Ps. 121:8). The brass doorknob is huge, as large as my outstretched hand.

"Gallicantu" in the church's name means "rooster crowing." Stained glass on the church depicts the moment Peter denied the Lord. On top of the church, higher than its cross—I loved this—stands a golden rooster! I'll never look at a weathervane the same again. How would you like to have a church built to commemorate your weakest moment? Not to mention having all four Gospels record it?

Three times Peter denied knowing the Lord—the last time with curses. And when the rooster crowed, Jesus looked directly at Peter—and their eyes met. Peter recalled the Lord's ominous prediction (see Luke 22:61; Matt. 26:75; Mark 14:72), and the devastated apostle once again took to foot, this time through a blur of bitter tears.

"Are You the Christ, the Son of the Blessed One?" Caiaphas pointed his bony finger at Jesus (Mark 14:61).

"I am," Jesus bluntly revealed, "and 'you shall see the Son of Man sitting at the right hand of power, and coming with the clouds of heaven'" (Mark 14:62). In other words, Jesus told them that He *was* the Messiah and that one day He would sit in judgment over them who judged Him. That cinched it.

Caiaphas ripped his own clothes, indicating he had heard the unthinkable. "What further need do we have of witnesses?" the high priest exploded. "You have heard the blasphemy; how does it seem to you?" (Mark 14:63-64). Both rhetorical questions, really—they had already decided to put Jesus to death.

However, as a nation occupied and governed by Rome, the Jews had no authority to carry out a death sentence. So after insulting and slapping Jesus around, and after issuing a perfunctory verdict in the Temple, Israel's religious leaders hauled Jesus to the Roman governor, Pontius Pilate, for condemnation.

The Citadel dominates the walls along the Old City's western side. Herod the Great built the bastion as his palace, a residence so ornate that the Jewish historian Josephus wrote, "[It] exceeds all my ability to describe it."[1] Standing on the Tower of Phasael, which Herod named after his brother, I looked south inside the walls of the fortress and could see archaeological remains that dated as far back as the time of Herod. (The picture on the cover of this book captures this view.) The king's extensive palace stretched from today's Jaffa Gate almost the entire length of the Armenian Quarter. The Citadel houses an excellent museum that outlines the complex history of Jerusalem; it took me hours to walk through it one day.

From the time the Romans began to govern Israel in A.D. 6, the Roman governor, or procurator, resided in the lavish palace whenever he visited Jerusalem.[2] (Otherwise, he normally resided in Caesarea.) Because Pontius Pilate stayed at the palace, or Praetorium, he probably judged Jesus here rather than at the Antonia Fortress, as some believe (a common misconception whose tradition is hard to uproot; see Mark 15:16; John 18:28).

"What accusation do you bring against this Man?" Pilate questioned the Jewish leaders (John 18:29).

"We found this man misleading our nation and forbidding to pay taxes to Caesar, and saying that He Himself is Christ, a King" (Luke 23:2). Their last charge, the only one Christ had done, Pilate seized upon. He turned to Jesus.

"Are You the King of the Jews?"

"It is as you say," Jesus affirmed (Luke 23:3).

Pilate looked at the chief priests. "I find no guilt in this man" (Luke 23:4; see also John 18:38; 19:4).

But they kept pressing, and in so doing Pilate discovered that Jesus hailed from Galilee. Like a good politician, Pilate passed the buck to the one who had jurisdiction over Galilee and who happened to be in Jerusalem during Passover—Herod Antipas.

A son of Herod the Great, Antipas had beheaded John the Baptist at the beginning of Jesus' ministry—a foreshadowing of how Jesus' ministry would end. Antipas had issued a phony threat on Jesus' life a year earlier, to which Jesus responded by calling him a "fox" (Luke 13:32). Jesus' use of the term referred to Antipas as insignificant, powerless, undignified and deceitful.[3] When Jesus stood before the king, who wanted only to see Jesus do a magic show, the Lord spoke what Antipas deserved to hear—nothing.

When Jesus again faced Pilate, the procurator did all he could to convince the Jewish leaders that he found no basis of guilt in Jesus. "What shall I do with Jesus who is called Christ?" (Matt. 27:22).

"Crucify Him!" they clamored.

"Why, what evil has He done?" (v. 23).

But they kept shouting, "Crucify Him!"

Hoping to appease the leaders, Pilate had Jesus scourged—a brutal act of whipping a prisoner with leather straps embedded with bits of bone and metal. The scourging typically ripped flesh from the body, leaving bones and innards exposed. Many prisoners died in the process.

To mock Jesus as the pitiful Jewish King, the Roman soldiers pressed a crown of thorns on His head and draped a purple robe over His mutilated body. Pilate then presented Jesus to the chief priests and crowds again. A collective gasp must have risen from the people.

"Behold, the Man!" Pilate pointed to Jesus (John 19:5).

I walked along the street parallel with the Temple Mount's northern wall and noticed a structure I had seen many times in pictures. The Ecce Homo Arch, a Latin name that translates Pilate's words "Behold, the Man!" allegedly represents the place where Pilate presented Jesus to the Jews (see John 19:4-5). The arch passes through a wall and touches the ground inside the adjacent Monastery of the Flagellation.

I entered the monastery and passed through a small museum into a large room with a low ceiling. Carefully placed lighting highlighted smooth stone slabs that were once part of an ancient pavement. Handrails in the middle of the room formed a rectangle, protecting something on the floor. I walked closer.

Our guide pointed to etchings in the stone floor and identified them as an ancient makeshift game board for the "King Game." The game's rules involved rolling dice; whoever landed on the crown first, won. Even though this pavement dates to a time later than that of Christ, if the Roman soldiers who crucified Jesus had this game in mind, it may have inspired their cruel mocking.

"Crucify, crucify!" the chief priests and their officers continued to demand (John 19:6). Rome declared Jesus innocent six times, but justice played no role in the process. "Away with Him, away with Him, crucify Him!" (John 19:15).

Pilate parleyed, "Shall I crucify your King?" (v. 15).

"We have no king but Caesar," snapped the chief priests. Oh, what a statement.

Those words represented the official rejection of Jesus. They refused the King whom God had sent them—along with the Kingdom He offered—and opted instead for a king like all the other nations. They proved themselves no different from Israel of old.

Pilate handed Jesus over to be crucified.

—⁂—

I left the monastery and the area of the Antonia Fortress, at the northwest corner of the Temple Mount, and headed west along the Via Dolorosa.

This famous "Way of Suffering" finds its basis in tradition, not history. Even though history points to the Citadel as the Praetorium, tradition often overshadows truth. The Via Dolorosa's present route, decided on only in the eighteenth century, serves as but a symbol of the true route Jesus walked to His crucifixion.

Every Good Friday, a procession of pilgrims carries crosses along the first 9 of 14 "stations" where, according to tradition, events on Jesus' route occurred. Some stations have a stone relief that depicts its significance. At Station 3, for instance, I saw a relief of Jesus falling under His cross for the first time. Other stations simply have roman numerals on the wall and expect you to know each number's significance.

The narrow processional route in the Old City opens into a wide courtyard with high walls all around. The courtyard is somewhat square, half as big as a basketball court, with several broad levels descending to the entrance of an ancient church.

When I was there, a number of religious-looking men meandered in the space. One looked like Friar Tuck, complete with brown robe and a white rope fixed around his waist. He ambled alongside another monk, who clutched a small book in his hands. On the east side of the square, an elderly Greek Orthodox priest sat in a red plastic chair before a door, somberly observing the goings-on. His snow-white beard covered his chest and much of his blue-black frock. He wore a dark smokestack hat with a small brim at

153

the top; it looked like Abraham Lincoln's hat worn upside down. A young priest approached him, dressed in all black and sporting a beard so thick it almost hid his face. (*Fuzz with eyeballs*, I thought.) The older evidently instructed the younger, who nodded incessantly. They exchanged a smile before the younger disappeared behind the door. At that moment, the older priest happened to look my way and our eyes met. His leftover smile dropped instantly into his previous somber stare.

Tourism first boomed in the Holy Land early in the fourth century, after the Roman Empire under Constantine adopted Christianity as its official religion. The emperor's mother, Helena, came to Palestine and asked local Christians—who had an unbroken presence in Jerusalem since Jesus' day—to locate sites for key biblical events. They pointed to the ground beneath Hadrian's pagan temple (built in A.D. 135) as the location of Jesus' death and burial. When workers dismantled the temple and removed the fill dirt of its foundation, Eusebius, the first biblical geographer, saw the tomb of Jesus come into view and described it as exhilarating.[4] Constantine erected a church over the site, but in 1009, the Egyptian ruler al-Hakim razed the church and had the tomb of Christ hacked down to bedrock. Much of the church I saw before me came from the time of the Crusades.

In the corner of the courtyard, I counted six crosses stacked in the corner from a recent procession down the Via Dolorosa. The remaining stations occurred within the church—the only section of the Via Dolorosa that parallels history.

No matter how hard I prepare myself, I always feel a spooky, spiritual strain in the Church of the Holy Sepulcher. Mostly because if I had to build a church over where Christ died and rose again, it would be nothing like the ornamental, almost ostentatious interior I saw. Today, six sects of Christendom jealously play a tug-of-war over who controls what in the church—so much so that a neutral Arab has to keep the key. The church seemed to represent the very hypocrisy Christ spoke against.

But again, in my own way, I have obscured the resurrection of Christ as well. By my own ornamental and ostentatious hypocrisy—

when I don't live as I know I should—the world sees the show and misses the Savior.

To me, the hypocrisy of the church's interior verifies the reason Christ died to begin with: Religion can't save us. So . . . maybe it fits after all.

I entered the church and ascended the stairs to the right, where tradition says the cross of Christ stood. Icons, incense, candles, chanting and traditionalism filled the tiny chapel, stifling any opportunity for me to meditate. I shared the small space with the usual line of worshippers who sequentially kissed the spot above the rock where the cross stood. With all the commotion, only a healthy imagination could picture the original scene, best with eyes closed.

In the first three hours on the cross—with spikes piercing His hands and feet, and puss oozing from the raw inflammations on His back—Jesus' only words revealed concern for others. He forgave a criminal dying beside Him, entrusted His mother into John's care and looked on His murderers with compassion: "Father, forgive them; for they do not know what they are doing" (Luke 23:34).

Their words, however, revealed different hearts. "Let this Christ, the King of Israel, now come down from the cross," the chief priests and the scribes mocked, "so that we may see and believe!" (Mark 15:31-32). "He saved others; He cannot save Himself!" they blasted.

Such an accusation carried the assumption that because He can save Himself, He should. It's almost like when Satan tempted Jesus to turn stones to bread and immediately remove the suffering that obedience required (see chapter 2). But now the stakes were higher: Jesus could take a shortcut and get the glory without the full suffering on the cross.

Darkness shrouded Jerusalem during Jesus' final three hours of life. During this time, the Gospels record absolutely nothing spoken— until the very end. The darkness reflected the unimaginable, spiritual agony Jesus endured.

"My God, my God, why have You forsaken Me?" (Matt. 27:46). In that moment, Jesus entered into spiritual death—that is, separation from the Father. Never in all eternity had Jesus endured this incomprehensible severance. But He willingly embraced it, knowing that the penalty for the sins of all humanity received its atonement then and there.

Right in front of where I stood, the New Covenant began, the universe was redeemed, and every sin I ever committed was paid for. I thought of some of them.

"It is finished!" Jesus shouted (John 19:30). He raised Himself against the nails to draw a final breath. "Father, into Your hands I commit My spirit" (Luke 23:46). Even in the blur of His pain and in the agony of spiritual death, Jesus entrusted His destiny to the Father's will.

Jesus' body fell limp, motionless and silent.

In that instant—a mere 300 yards east—the Temple experienced *anything* but silence. A deafening rip filled the courts as the veil that separated mankind from the Holy of Holies tore in two from top to bottom (see Mark 15:38). Like the sky that "tore" open above Jesus' baptism, so the renting of the veil revealed the Father's acceptance of Jesus' death on our behalf; in fact, Mark used this Greek term only those two times (see Mark 1:10).

It was as if the Father gave His approval again: "You are My beloved Son, in You I am well-pleased" (Mark 1:11). Centuries of sacrifices—burnt offerings wafting their pleasing aroma heavenward—found ultimate fulfillment in the flawless sacrifice of Jesus (see Eph. 5:2).

If you think about it, the New Testament does not begin with Matthew chapter 1—at least, not theologically. Remember Jesus' words upstairs? "This cup which is poured out for you is the new covenant in My blood" (Luke 22:20). The New Covenant, long promised from Jeremiah 31:31-34, began with the shed blood of Jesus. When we think of the transition between the Old and New Testaments (or Covenants), we should understand it as occurring at the *end* of the Gospels rather than at the beginning. Jesus was born under the Law and fulfilled its demands by His perfect life and His innocent death (see Gal. 4:4; Heb. 9:11-14; 10:19-20).

The tearing of the veil meant that all the elaborate rituals required in the wilderness Tabernacle and the Jerusalem Temples had been satisfied once and for all in Jesus Christ (see 1 Pet. 3:18). Even though Israel of old did experience the benefits of atonement on credit, the centuries of animal sacrifices did not pay for sin—they only delayed payment.

The final bill came due on the cross (see Rom. 4:25). Now Christ offers forgiveness to anyone who believes in Him.

But these great truths and their reasons for hope had not yet come to light.

When Joseph of Arimathea requested Jesus' body from the cross and laid it in his own new tomb nearby, it was as if all the dreams that surrounded this dead Messiah now lay buried alongside His lifeless corpse (see Mark 15:43-46). The huge, immovable stone before the entrance seemed to entomb the potential for all future hope. Death feels so unforgiving and final.

The sorrow that hung over the disciples' hearts felt heavier than the black skies that hovered over Jerusalem. The darkness that began at noon perhaps extended throughout the evening until night consumed it. As the disillusioned disciples cowered in dark corners, they may have wondered if the sun would ever shine again.

—⁓—

157

Roosters don't observe the Sabbath, it turns out.

Peter would have awakened Saturday morning to the loud, repetitive and humiliating reminder of his denial of Jesus and of the Savior's piercing gaze. The reality of facing every morning for the rest of his life with a raucous flashback of his failure must have seemed unbearable. Just when Peter thought he could weep no more, the bitter tears must have flowed again down a face wrinkled with regret.

No doubt Saturday dragged long in the thoughts of Jesus' disciples. The Sabbath allowed for no work or considerable activity. It was as if God's Law forced on them a time to sit and think . . . and lament their failures. The cross had thrust them into the ugly face of their misplaced hopes for glory.

Jesus would show them that the Messiah didn't fail their expectations. Quite the opposite! Their own expectations had failed them.

It's the same with us.

I think when we find ourselves most disappointed with life, it's not because something in life has failed us. Rather, our expectations of what life "ought to be" have failed us. Or understood a different way, when we find ourselves most disappointed with God, God has not failed us—*our expectations of God have failed us.*

Sometimes when our faith is too weak to trust God, He puts us in a place where our weakness forces us to surrender. Not to trust, but to surrender. Surrender then lays the groundwork for trust, because God always shows Himself faithful.

The shattered disciples had built their hopes on their own dreams of glory and greatness and not on what Jesus had told them (see Luke 24:13-27). Greatness in God's eyes comes through living with a servant's heart—the kind of life Jesus had modeled in His life and in His death. Though they had walked in the footsteps of Jesus for years, they had failed to hear His words. Even being upstairs with Jesus and eating the Passover lamb had failed to open their eyes. It took the cross.

Jesus clearly foretold His death to His men—and it unfolded with all the uncompromising precision He predicted. But His death wasn't all He promised. It was only the beginning.

In creating the world, God ceased working on the Sabbath, or Saturday. That means that God *began* creation on a Sunday morning, the same day of the week Jesus rose from the dead. "For God, who said, 'Let light shine out of darkness,' made his light shine in our hearts to give us the light of the knowledge of the glory of God in the face of Christ" (2 Cor. 4:6, *NIV*).

The next morning as the sun pierced the darkness, Peter's rooster would crow again, announcing a very, very different new day.

Notes

1. Flavius Josephus and William Whiston, *The Works of Josephus: Complete and Unabridged*, Wars 5.176 (1987; Peabody: Hendrickson, 1996).

2. Jerome Murphy-O'Connor, *The Holy Land: An Oxford Archaeological Guide from Earliest Times to 1700*, 4th ed. (New York: Oxford University Press, 1998), p. 22.

3. Harold W. Hoehner, *Herod Antipas: A Contemporary of Jesus Christ* (Grand Rapids, MI: Academie Books/Zondervan Publishing House, 1972), p. 347.

4. Eusebius, *Church History, Life of Constantine the Great, and Oration in Praise of Constantine*, vol. 3, p. 28, quoted in Phillip Schaff and Henry Wace, eds., *Nicene and Post-Nicene Fathers, Second Series*, vol. 1, American reprint ed. (Peabody, MA: Hendrickson, 1994), p. 527.

CHAPTER EIGHT

A TOMB WITH A VIEW

"He is not here, for He has risen, just as He said.
Come, see the place where He was lying."
MATTHEW 28:6

"Holy place. No shorts."

The sign welcomed us back to Tabgha, beside the Sea of Galilee.

The church I entered, the size of a gymnasium, covers a number of Byzantine mosaics. Its most famous design commemorates Jesus' multiplication of the loaves and fishes—the event from which this church gets its name (though the miracle occurred elsewhere; see chapter 4). Candles flickered here and there, with unlit ones available for purchase.

Not far down the road, a narrow footpath led us to a modest structure made of old gray blocks. The Franciscan chapel had only a dozen seats facing an altar up front. The sign on the bare rock beneath the altar read "Mensa Christi," meaning "Table of Christ." A painting on the wall depicted Peter dressed like the pope, prostrate before Jesus. I could hear the rhythmic waves lapping against the shoreline outside the Church of the Primacy of St. Peter.

The bare rock under the altar extended under and outside the chapel wall. I walked outside and saw a rusted gate that fenced off the rock with yet another sign on top: "This is a Holy Ground."

The naturally rocky shoreline I had seen years earlier now had leveled pea gravel to accommodate elderly tourists. I stooped where the waves slapped the shore and I withdrew a stone from the Sea of Galilee. The constant lapping had hollowed holes in the rock, and the algae that greened my fingers reminded me of the nearby springs—and why this spot has remained a mainstay for fishermen for thousands of years. Peter knew it well.

"I'm going out to fish," Simon Peter muttered to six of the other disciples (John 21:3, *NIV*).

159

"We'll go with you," they answered (John 21:3, *NIV*). But they didn't catch anything that night.

Sunrise on the Sea of Galilee flattens all objects into silhouettes and paints the sky a murky red. As the sun peeks over the eastern hills, it draws a line of light from the distant shore straight across the water to wherever you stand—and follows you like a spotlight.

As daybreak began to warm the disciples' backs, no doubt a few roosters responded to instinct. Peter continued to pull in his nets without a word. A lone figure appeared on the shore about a hundred yards away and called out to the men.

"Friends, haven't you any fish?" (John 21:5, *NIV*).

"No," they grunted.

"Throw your net on the right side of the boat and you will find some" (v. 6). As ridiculous as it sounded, they did it. The immediate, enormous catch could only mean one thing.

"It is the Lord!" John whooped (v. 7). *Splash!* Peter started to swim the length of a football field straight toward Jesus.

I stood next to the "Holy Ground" rock where Jesus had called out to the disciples, and I pictured the boat and silhouette of Peter thrashing his way toward me. Peter may have remembered, as I did, the angel's words to the women that first Easter Sunday sunrise in Jerusalem: "He has risen; He is not here; behold, here is the place where they laid Him. But go, tell His disciples and Peter, 'He is going ahead of you to Galilee; there you will see Him, just as He told you'" (Mark 16:6-7).

"And Peter," the angel had added—those blessed two words! Swimming as fast as he had sprinted to the empty tomb, Peter never took his eyes off Jesus (see John 20:3-8). This wasn't the first time Jesus appeared to Peter after the resurrection (see John 21:14; 1 Cor. 15:5), but it was the first time they met in Galilee. Jesus had kept His promise to meet the disciples there.

But the location Jesus chose should have arrested Peter's thoughts with its implications. Years earlier, beside these same waters at Tabgha, a dumbfounded Peter had fallen at Jesus' feet after a miraculous catch of fish (see chapter 3). Peter's confession to Jesus back then must also have mirrored how he felt now: "Go away from me, Lord, for I am a sinful man!" (see Luke 5:1-8).

As the exhausted disciple slogged ashore, he must have collapsed and pooled water at Jesus' feet—in a way, like the painting I had seen in the chapel. *Well, sort of.*

When the other disciples reached shore with the miraculous catch in tow, they found a charcoal fire already laid, with fish cooking on the Mensa Christi. Can you imagine eating a meal Jesus had made?

"Come and have breakfast," Jesus invited (John 21:12).

Even though Peter was warming himself at the fire, his mind must have been swimming with the scene Jesus had set up. The props were unmistakable: the miraculous catch at Tabgha, the sunrise . . . and those blasted roosters. But one more cue confirmed Jesus' intent that morning: the charcoal fire.

The only other time the Greek term for "charcoal fire" appears in the whole New Testament occurs three chapters earlier, where we read that Peter warmed himself in Caiaphas's courtyard—and denied Jesus (see John 18:18; 21:9). And now Peter sat in an awkward déjà vu.

After breakfast, as the day began to brighten, Jesus and Peter took a walk.[1] The Lord had a question to ask, and He called Peter by the same name as when they had first met. "Simon, son of John, do you love Me more than these?" (John 21:15).

"Yes, Lord," Peter replied. "You know that I love You."

Three times Jesus questioned Peter's love, and three times Peter affirmed it. It hurt Peter the third time Jesus asked the question— perhaps because of the way Jesus asked it or because Peter finally connected it with his threefold denial of Christ. Peter answered with sincerity: "Lord, You know all things; You know that I love You" (v. 17).

After every assertion of Peter's love, Jesus responded with a command: "Tend My lambs. . . . Shepherd My sheep. . . . Tend My sheep" (John 21:15-17). In other words, love for Christ translates into serving others—the very lesson Jesus had taught them in the Upper Room. Peter would later exhort his readers with these same words (see 1 Pet. 5:1-3).

Jesus could have taken Peter back to Bethsaida for this conversation. It would have made sense, wouldn't it? Near Bethsaida, Jesus had taught the people "because they were like sheep without a shepherd" (Matt. 9:36). Bethsaida would have reminded Peter that the *way* to feed Jesus' sheep and shepherd His flock comes from constant dependence on Jesus—even when you have only a few loaves and fish to work with (see chapter 4). At Bethsaida, Jesus had taught them *how* to do ministry. But instead, the Lord wanted to remind Peter *why* to do ministry.

When they first met, Peter had walked with Jesus out of a motive for glory and a prime seat in the kingdom of God. But now, Peter would follow out of gratitude for God's grace—out of love.

After Peter affirmed his devotion for Christ, the Lord revealed what that love would cost him: "When you were younger," Jesus looked at Peter, "you used to gird yourself and walk wherever you wished; but when you grow old, you will stretch out your hands and someone else will gird you, and bring you where you do not wish to go" (John 21:18). In other words, Jesus told Peter that he would die a martyr's death—the very thing Peter had feared when he denied Jesus. "Follow Me!" Jesus added, again reminding the apostle of their beginnings together (Mark 1:17; John 21:19).

Peter noticed John walking behind them. "Lord, and what about this man?" (John 21:21). Having learned of his own violent death, Peter inquired how John would die. *Torture? Crucifixion? Come on, Lord, You can tell me!* Peter still struggled with comparisons. Jesus' response brought Peter's priorities back into perspective.

"If I want him to remain until I come, what is that to you?" Then Jesus repeated the command, with a particular emphasis, "*You* follow Me!" (John 21:22, emphasis added). Just as we reveal our love for Jesus by serving others, so we should serve without comparing ourselves to others.

Someone else's calling or cross always seems a better deal than ours. But answer Jesus' question, "What is that to you?" Jesus died for all of us at once; but we enter a relationship with Him as individuals: "*You* follow Me!"

When we compare our lot with that of others, we forget that God saved us when He was obligated only to judge our sin. We forget that our motivation for following Jesus is love for Him—not what we get from Him. The apostle Paul would later write to Christians who struggled with comparisons: "When they measure themselves by themselves and compare themselves with themselves, they are not wise" (2 Cor. 10:12, *NIV*).

The bottom line? Comparison stems from either coveting or pride and smacks of basic ingratitude to God.

Jesus took Simon Peter back to Tabgha—to the place where their relationship first began, to the place of grace, where a miraculous catch had pulled from Peter a confession: "I am a sinful man!" There Jesus reinstated Peter and reminded him of his purpose. Now the roosters would become a reminder of God's forgiveness rather than a flashback of Peter's failure. Grace often brings ironic blessings, doesn't it?

Christ reminded Peter what all Christians should remember: Our relationship with Jesus expresses itself by serving others without comparing ourselves with them. And the motivation for such devotion? Jesus answered that with a question.

163

"Do you truly love Me?"

—⚏—

The northwest corner of the Sea of Galilee has a sheer rock cliff, recognizable from most any spot on the lake. Rising over 1,300 feet above the water, Mount Arbel stands like a sentinel over the northern shore. I always enjoy knowing that I see the cliff as Jesus saw it. Geography doesn't move.

But the best way to enjoy Mount Arbel is to go to the top of it. The panoramic view astounds every first-timer. But if you go, you may need to cling to the lone tree up there—as well as to your hat. It's windy!

Part of the International Highway ran along the broad plain below where I stood on Mount Arbel—roughly where the modern road runs today. I thought of all the armies of history that had marched right below me. They would have used Mount Arbel as a familiar landmark in their journeys.

And though the history intrigues and the view inspires, the greatest benefit I've enjoyed from the top of Arbel comes as I see—from one location—the places where Jesus spent most of His ministry: Capernaum, the Cove of the Sower, the Mount of Beatitudes, Tabgha—these and other places lie almost in a line along the shore.

For this reason, I wonder in pure conjecture if "the mountain" to which Jesus brought His disciples for the Great Commission was Mount Arbel (Matt. 28:16). It really could have been. From here they could see the Sea of Galilee, where Jesus had commanded the wind and the waves, and Capernaum, where He had demonstrated His heavenly authority by teaching and performing miracles. They could see the place where Jesus had called them as disciples. And they could observe the highway that led to the nations.

Got the picture? Now read Jesus' words to them with this setting in mind: "All authority has been given to Me in heaven and on earth. Go therefore and make disciples of all the nations, baptizing them in the name of the Father and the Son and the Holy Spirit, teaching them to observe all that I commanded you; and lo, I am with you always, even to the end of the age" (Matt. 28:18-20).

They had the message, but they still lacked the power to give it. Time to head back to Jerusalem.

We most often quote the Great Commission Jesus gave in Galilee. But He repeated it, probably a number of times, as He appeared to His apostles "over a period of forty days," during which time He continually verified His bodily resurrection to them—and taught them "of the things concerning the kingdom of God" (see Acts 1:3).

Ah, yes, the kingdom of God. Now it made sense! Or so they thought. Jesus had died and risen, so now the Kingdom can come! (And of course, the apostles can now sit on their thrones as well.) But just to be sure, they asked about it as they stood with Him atop the Mount of Olives beside Jerusalem.

"Lord, is it at this time You are restoring the kingdom to Israel?" (Acts 1:6). "It is not for you to know times or epochs which the Father has fixed by His own authority," Jesus answered (v. 7).

They had another task Jesus had given them, but they still lacked the power to do it. When they had been upstairs with Jesus, He had promised that though He would leave, He would not leave them alone. The Holy Spirit, who had descended on Jesus at His baptism and who had empowered the Son of God to teach and do miracles, would be sent by Jesus as a "Helper" so that the apostles could do ministry as well (see John 14:16-17). And from the inspiration of the Holy Spirit, the final books of Scripture would come through some of these same men (see John 16:12-15; 2 Pet. 1:20-21; 3:15-16).

In His earthly life, Jesus "tabernacled" with us as part of God's unfolding plan to dwell with His children. But the Holy Spirit took this to another level still—He *indwells* God's children. The physical body of every Christian now represents "a temple of the Holy Spirit who is in you, whom you have from God" (1 Cor. 6:19). The Spirit's indwelling fulfills God's promise to "dwell in them and walk among them" (2 Cor. 6:16; cf. Lev. 26:12; 1 Cor. 3:16; Eph. 2:18-22). But God's *ultimate* dwelling with His own in the New Heaven and New Earth completes what the earthly Tabernacle and Temple only foreshadowed: "Behold, the tabernacle of God is among men, and He shall dwell among them, and they shall be His people, and God Himself shall be among them" (Rev. 21:3).

Forever, we'll be camping with Jesus.

Just before ascending to heaven, Jesus promised the Spirit's power to the disciples—interestingly, in terms similar to Gabriel's announcement of Mary's miraculous conception. "But you will receive power when the Holy Spirit has come upon you; and you shall be My witnesses both in Jerusalem, and in all Judea and Samaria, and even to the remotest part of the earth" (Acts 1:8; cf. Luke 1:35).

"One day you're an unbeliever," my Jewish friend Amir spoke of his conversion, "and the next day you're a preacher!" When Amir saw the *Jesus* film in Jerusalem and accepted Christ, he immediately went home to tell his nine brothers about it.

"I was sitting around the table with all my foster brothers, and I wanted everybody to know the Lord—except one. One I really couldn't stand. But God has a sense of humor, because of all people around the table, the only one who responded was him! Both of us started going to prayer meetings, Bible studies and worship services. Until one day we came home and my foster family told both of us: 'Take your things and get out of here.'" God used their rejection to guide Amir further into His perfect will for him.

Persecution scattered Jesus' disciples as well—into Judea and Samaria and to the remotest parts of the earth. God would even take one of the vilest persecutors, Saul of Tarsus, and convert him into the most powerful Christian missionary the world has ever seen.

Jesus' short-term mission trip to Earth stamped the imprint of His own passport on the hearts of every follower of Christ. "As the Father has sent me," He told His disciples, "I also send you" (John 20:21). In other words, the mission trip the Father sent Jesus on, Jesus now sends us to continue.

—◆—

166

The early morning sun rested three fingers above the horizon, rising to the right of our southbound vessel. I sat alone on the deck of the *Wind Spirit* with a cup of coffee and my Bible. Cool breezes carried no scent of the salt sea in the air. As far as I could see, the skies proclaimed the work of God's hands. Other than a few of the crew chatting some distance away, I could hear nothing but the steady sound of the ship's motor as we cut a wide wake in the blue Aegean Sea.

Our visit to Ephesus in Turkey the day before seemed surreal—and so very far from the land of Israel. We had explored the extensive ruins with its paved streets and stone buildings that boasted over a quarter of a million people in the apostle Paul's day. We had entered the 25,000-seat theater and had sung a hymn to God where the silversmiths had shouted praise to the goddess Artemis in riot against Paul's ministry (see Acts 19:28-32).

But what I had found most fascinating about Ephesus was at the end of the road that began just outside the theater. Called the Arcadian Way, this street served as the main thoroughfare from the harbor to the city; Ephesus lay along major caravan routes from the east and its harbor provided shipping routes to the west. I paced down the street toward the ancient harbor, past the usual right turn toward the exit, and walked as far as the street would allow. I looked in every direction . . . but no sea.

Centuries of silt from the Cayster River had accumulated in the harbor and gradually pushed the waterfront away from the city. The citizens had tried to restrain the silting, but they eventually had given up. Today the ruins of Ephesus sit about *five miles* from the Aegean Sea! Grain after grain of silt, year after year of deposits, finally reduced a city of great influence to insignificance.

A small Turkish village squats on part of the site of ancient Ephesus today. The town's name, Ayasaluk, corrupts two Greek words that refer to another apostle of Ephesus, *hagios theologos*—"the holy divine."[2] History reveals that the aging apostle John settled in Ephesus long after Paul had founded the church and ministered there.

Standing next to the Byzantine basilica that honors John, we had looked at the quagmire where the Temple of Artemis once stood, one of the Seven Wonders of the Ancient World. Only a single, crumbling column from the temple stands there today—with a stork's nest on top! I remembered seeing several of the pristine original columns in the Hagia Sophia Church in Istanbul, where the Emperor Justinian had moved them in the sixth century.

Although John would eventually return and die in Ephesus, Domitian banished him in A.D. 95 to a small island to the southwest. And this morning, our vessel was headed that direction.

The Aegean Sea parted against our hull as we made our way from the coast of Kusadasi, Turkey, to the northwest end of the Dodecanese Islands. We pulled into the narrow isthmus that divides the island of Patmos in half and serves as its harbor. The *Wind Spirit* anchored offshore and we boarded a tender for port.

On our way in to the docks, the island's terrain reminded me of what I saw on scuba diving trips to Cozumel, Mexico. The blue sea looked like Disneyworld water, but the island itself looked scrubby and primitive. Once ashore, we chartered a motor coach and snaked uphill along winding roads with breathtaking views of the island and

Christian symbols that archaeologists
discovered at Ephesus.

Atop Mount Arbel in Israel, overlooking the ancient International Highway and the north shore of the Sea of Galilee, where Jesus spent much of His ministry.

Sunset over the Island of Patmos,
as seen from the Aegean Sea.

the Aegean. As we neared the top, I saw a row of discarded toilets on the hillside to my left. I couldn't resist and quipped to two friends: "Those must be the Saint Johns."

We pulled into the Monastery of Saint John and descended several flights of steep steps. A familiar sign, "No photographs," welcomed us to the Holy Cave of the Apocalypse—where tradition says John received the book of Revelation.

The cave seemed hardly a cave—more like an enclosed depression in the hill. The small room had a single window on the left and an altar in front, with about a dozen empty seats facing it. Beneath a low-hanging outcropping of rock to my right, a small cloth hung on the bare cave wall.

A priest, dressed head to foot in holy garb, eyed those of us with cameras and scrutinized our motives the whole time. His critical gaze irritated me at first, but I determined to return his glare with kindness.

"Hello, good morning," I told him genuinely. He nodded abruptly and looked away with a deadpan face.

"Please sit," came another voice. Our group began to fill in the seats. I stood in the back as another priest began his talk.

"This is the cave where John received the Revelation." He then pointed to the outcropping. "You can see where the rock split three ways when God called to John, indicating the three Persons of the Trinity." He pointed first to the floor and said, "John slept here," and then to an indentation in the wall, "and being an old man, he put his hand here to help himself up." Finally, the priest walked to the slanted cave wall draped with a cloth. "Here John wrote the Revelation."

Good grief, I thought. I half expected to be shown outside where he relieved himself.

Okay, so maybe all these details are correct. Don't *I* also get excited in Israel when I see somewhere I *know* an event took place? Don't I also at times venerate the trivial and ignore the essential? Absolutely.

I thought of John's words in the book of Revelation, perhaps received in this cave: "Blessed is he who reads and those who hear the words of the prophecy, *and heed the things which are written in it*, for the time is near" (Rev. 1:3, emphasis added). Pointing to John's handhold in the wall should do more for us than give us tingles. It's not even enough to read and hear what John wrote. We must *heed the word*.

We must live it.

After the brief lecture, I walked over to the window that would have been John's view out of the cave and cast a glance across the azure Aegean Sea. I pictured myself as John, an old man. Most likely in Ephesus, the aged apostle had already written the inspired Gospel that bears his name. I'm sure he shook his head or his eyes welled up—or both—as he inked his quill and remembered Christ's wise and patient words, his own immaturities, and the long years it took to get the glory-seeking arrogance out of his pursuits.

All those days and nights John spent with Jesus, with so many opportunities to talk with Him about things that really mattered. But instead, out came questions like, "Lord, do You want us to command fire to come down from heaven and consume them?" (Luke 9:54); and statements like, "Teacher, we saw someone casting out demons in Your name, and we tried to prevent him because he was not following us" (Mark 9:38); and of course, "Teacher, we want You to do for us whatever we ask of You" (Mark 10:35).

The long days on Patmos must have seemed terribly sentimental as John remembered the events with Jesus that had transpired over five decades earlier. I wonder if he felt privileged or guilty about his old age when all the other disciples—every one—had died a martyr's death. John had outrun Peter to the tomb, but Peter had beaten John to heaven. His own brother James had gulped Christ's cup of suffering in a quick execution (see Acts 12:2), but John sipped it slowly in lonely places of exile (see Rev. 1:9).

Then one Sunday on Patmos, the resurrected Jesus appeared to John and told him to pick up his quill again. "Write in a book what you see, and send it to the seven churches" (Rev. 1:11). The first of those letters went to John's familiar city—Ephesus.

—⁓—

Ruins of Ephesus descending to the ancient, silted harbor.

Island of Patmos harbor, viewed from the Monastery of Saint John.

What if God inspired three books of Scripture for your church and also sent two apostles to minister among you for years? Ephesus got both.

The apostle Paul devoted three years as a missionary living in Ephesus. Later, when imprisoned in Rome, Paul penned the book of Ephesians to this vibrant church. Paul also would write two letters to Timothy, the church's pastor. Finally, the apostle John lived there and probably wrote the Gospel of John before his exile to Patmos. What great teaching Ephesus received!

No wonder Jesus commended them as John wrote to them from Patmos (see Rev. 2:1-3). They had stood firm in both their deeds and their doctrine for 30 years. Wonderful!

"But I have this against you," Jesus continued, "that you have left your first love" (Rev. 2:4).

Amazing—this church had received three books of Scripture and two resident apostles! While other churches struggled against heresy, Ephesus had guarded their deeds and doctrine. Yet they had failed to maintain their devotion. Moreover, they had left it.

I imagined myself standing again in Ephesus at the end of the Arcadian Way. The silting of the harbor had removed the city's economic influence, and now the Aegean Sea sits miles from the ruins.

I began to relate that silting to the spiritual life—the silting of the heart, not the harbor. Grain after grain of busyness, year after year of neglected devotion to Jesus, had finally reduced a church of such doctrinal strength to devotional attrition. The Ephesian Christians had lost their first love by allowing the silt of spiritual indifference to accumulate over the years. It can happen to anyone. Even to you and me.

Mind a few questions? When is the last time you talked with an unbeliever about Jesus? Or studied the Bible beyond simply reading it? What about just sitting in God's presence in silent worship? And the kicker: How's your prayer life?

Oh, that's what new *Christians do.* We're all tempted to think that, aren't we? And we're correct. But Jesus took it a step further: *That's what* Christians *do.*

As believers, we never outgrow the basics. We either build on them or abandon them. We can wake up after a number of years and discover that our lack of passion for Jesus has gradually silted Him five miles away from our hearts. We then find ourselves living in the ruins of once-vibrant spiritual lives. How does this happen?

Our hearts begin to silt when we content ourselves with maintaining a level of godliness that makes cultural Christianity our standard. In other words, compared to most Christians, like Jim or Susan or Pastor Ted, our spiritual life meets the standard. We seem in great shape. Our challenge has become spiritual maintenance rather than spiritual growth. And our hearts fill with silt without our knowing it.

But the pattern for the Christian life has never been other Christians—it is Christ. How easily we can forget that. Do we strive to become *like Him* or like our Christian culture? Do we give our all *to Him*—or do we just give what's necessary to keep up appearances? It takes guts to answer those questions honestly. It takes even more courage to change.

Like the Ephesians, we often feel that godly behavior and orthodox beliefs are all that God expects. But it isn't. Jesus Christ wants our *affections*—He wants to be our first love. In every situation in which we live and serve, in every action, our motive should find its root in love for Jesus. The goal is love, and love expresses itself in those ways we often confuse as the goal (see 1 Tim. 1:5). Loving God with all our heart, soul, mind and strength is still the greatest commandment (see Deut. 6:5; Luke 10:27).

"Remember from where you have fallen," Jesus told them, "and repent and do the deeds you did at first" (Rev. 2:5). Jesus always wants to take us back to where our relationship with Him began—back to our first love.

I think this is why Jesus took His disciples back to Galilee following His resurrection.

After John put down his quill from writing to the Ephesians, he might have closed his eyes and listened. Hearing the sound of the waves run ashore on Patmos, he could have imagined a different shore far away where Jesus had spoken to another who had lost his first love.

"Do you love Me?" Jesus' question came to Peter. And the question also comes to us.

Everybody wants to grow spiritually until we discover what growing costs us. When the difficulty of love and obedience really hits the Christian life, many stack their crosses in the corner of the courtyard and no longer walk the Via Dolorosa. Like those who hollered to Jesus as He hung dying, "Save Yourself, and come down from the cross!" (Mark 15:30), so we assume we shouldn't bear a cross either—and because Jesus *can* remove it, He *should*. We presume this, even though He has told us the exact opposite.

If we consider the life and ministry of Christ as we've followed Him through this book, we discover that God's pattern for shaping our lives mirrors Jesus' model in training the Twelve.

It begins with Jesus coming to us—camping with us—by becoming a man and taking our sin on Himself. He calls us to follow Him, and we do, dragging along our own hopes of what the Christian life will hold. But unavoidably, we come face to face with the reality of temptation and our false expectations. We thought Jesus would make life easier, even glorious, when in fact He has handed us a cross to shoulder—and given us His own servant example to follow.

We discover that our greatest need is mercy, not glory. We learn that our purpose in life—our joy in life—is to follow Jesus wherever He chooses, not to use Jesus to get where and what we want. "You have been called for this purpose," a transformed Peter would later write, "since Christ also suffered for you, leaving you an example for you to follow in His steps" (1 Pet. 2:21).

Jesus was willing to disappoint His disciples so that they would experience the joy of forgiveness of sin—a joy they did not even know to hope for in their blind zeal for glory. *Jesus was willing to disappoint everyone but the Father.* Ponder that for a moment. Jesus loved His own enough to disappoint them, to allow them to question His power and to struggle against their own weaknesses, in order that they could experience true joy in the long term.

Jesus is willing to disappoint you for the same reason.

Most often, spiritual growth comes only as a result of God thrusting us into places we would never go ourselves. In these places, He shows us who we really are—a dismal and disappointing revelation. But like Peter, the experience is a necessary reality. And yet, in these tough places, God also shows us who *He* really is—a discovery worth all the pain in the world (see Job 42:1-3). Neither lesson would we ever learn from the armchair. Or the pew. Or even the pulpit. We only learn it in the crucible of pain. But for the joy set before us, it is worth it.

I once heard Dr. Howard Hendricks say, "Sometimes we have to blast before we can build." When God blasts our false expectations, it's only so that He can build reality into our hearts. The blasting, as hard as it seems to understand—impossible sometimes—stems from His infinite love for us. Our response then becomes a greater love for Him (see 1 John 4:19).

—⁓—

After our ship pulled away from the island of Patmos, the place where God's revelation came to a close, I could still make out the Monastery of Saint John on top of a hill. Cathy and I sat on deck of the *Wind Spirit* and read portions of the book of Revelation while we looked at the very place where God inspired John to write it. In a few days, we would be home again, back to the ends of the earth where Christ commissioned us. Back to the crosses He has called us to bear. Back to the privilege of following Jesus.

I don't think it's enough to come to the lands of the Bible—or to the Bible itself—just to ask questions or to walk where Jesus walked. Questions about faith should never be simply rhetorical. They must have answers, and the answers must reveal themselves in a changed life. Our questions must also dig deeper to consider *why* we're willing to change.

"Do you love Me?"—Jesus already knows our answer. But He asks so that we may know. For therein lies our motivation.

The Aegean Sea beneath our hull and the Sea of Galilee that washed ashore at Tabgha both echoed in my mind. They reminded me of the probing words of Jesus, recorded through John's pen: "You have lost your first love." They remind me of Jesus' gracious command: "*You* follow Me."

My life must grow to where *all I do* flows from a love and an affection for Jesus, who died and rose and will return—out of love for me. What an unspeakable privilege to walk in His footsteps every day.

With the sun offering its last bits of light, I watched the island until it sank below our wake in the distant horizon.

Notes

1. I take it that Jesus and Peter went for a walk because Peter is described as "turning around" and seeing John "following them" (John 21:20).

2. M. G. Easton, *Easton's Bible Dictionary* (1897; Oak Harbor, WA: Logos Research Systems, Inc., 1996).

SCRIPTURE INDEX

180

SITE/SUBJECT INDEX

189

AUTHOR'S NOTE

Dear Friend,

Before you ever picked up this book, I prayed for you.

I prayed that the seeds it would plant in your heart would help you along the journey that God has for you as you walk in the footsteps of Jesus.

Feel free to visit my website for helpful links on including biblical geography and suggested resources in your study of God's Word. The site also contains articles, recommended links and a variety of content to encourage your spiritual journey at whatever stage you find yourself along the way.

For speaking engagements, questions or generally edifying comments, feel free to email me at the address below. I may not be able to respond to all mail personally, but I enjoy hearing from you.

Thank you for taking this journey with me,

Wayne Stiles
www.waynestiles.com